ROUTLEDGE LIBRARY EDITIONS:
CONSUMER BEHAVIOUR

Volume 6

# CAPITALISM AND THE CONSUMER

# CAPITALISM AND THE CONSUMER

FRED HENDERSON

Routledge
Taylor & Francis Group
LONDON AND NEW YORK

First published in 1936

This edition first published in 2015
by Routledge
2 Park Square, Milton Park, Abingdon, Oxon, OX14 4RN

and by Routledge
711 Third Avenue, New York, NY 10017

*Routledge is an imprint of the Taylor & Francis Group, an informa business*



*British Library Cataloguing in Publication Data*
A catalogue record for this book is available from the British Library

ISBN: 978-1-138-79276-0 (Set)
eISBN: 978-1-315-73357-9 (Set)
ISBN: 978-1-138-83275-6 (Volume 6)
eISBN: 978-1-315-73581-8 (Volume 6)

**Publisher's Note**
The publisher has gone to great lengths to ensure the quality of this reprint but points out that some imperfections in the original copies may be apparent.

**Disclaimer**
The publisher has made every effort to trace copyright holders and would welcome correspondence from those they have been unable to trace.

# CAPITALISM AND THE CONSUMER

*by*

FRED HENDERSON

LONDON

GEORGE ALLEN & UNWIN LTD

MUSEUM STREET

FIRST PUBLISHED IN 1936



PRINTED IN GREAT BRITAIN BY
UNWIN BROTHERS LTD., WOKING

# CAPITALISM AND THE CONSUMER

## CHAPTER ONE

A NEW definite formulation round a central purpose seems to be beginning in current economic thought and discussion. The famous speech in which the Governor of the Bank of England made frank confession to his fellow bankers—"The difficulties are so vast, the forces so unlimited, so novel, and precedents are so lacking, that I approach the whole subject not only in ignorance, but in humility: it is too great for me"—has been quoted often enough with the malicious intent of suggesting that it might serve as a fitting preface to everything our economists have had to offer us for dealing with our present confusions. And there has certainly been a good deal of justification for that gibe. There has been precious little sense of direction in the economic wisdom served up to us, and very little indication indeed of the centric kind of understanding from which any dependable sense of direction might issue. But now, it seems, a new definition of our problem in terms of central understanding is finding expression; and our current economic thinking tends to move into relation to it with all the appearance of natural gravitation to a real centric concept.

Mr. Roosevelt has given expression to it in his statement to the American people of the principle of action by which he suggests that any New Deal, if it is to be effective, must be governed. "We are," he says, "at the threshold of a fundamental change in our economic thought; in future we are going to think less about the producer and more about the consumer. . . . The millions who are in want will not stand silently by for ever while the things to satisfy their needs are within easy reach."

Consumer-economics: production for use: making the interests of the consumer dominant in economic policy—our current economic thinking, in its direction and outlook, begins everywhere to show this "fundamental change," as Mr. Roosevelt very truly describes it. That there should be such a general insurgence of this consumer-motive in our economic thought is not to be wondered at. For, once the thing finds expression, it is like a searchlight on our economic confusions; an illumination in which the present trouble of mankind stands unmistakably defined as the failure of our existing economy to function in the interest of the consumer.

It is not an isolated local or national trouble. Special national circumstances may modify it in minor details; but in its underlying reality what is happening to the life of the world is the same thing and presents the same problem everywhere. It is just this—that the peoples of the world are being disabled from getting into use and consumption the things they all want and can produce in abundance. Our need for the things is urgent; our power to produce them is ample; but for some reason not yet detected by the governing statesmanship of the world we are having to go without them.

Whatever difficulty statesmanship may find in detecting the causes of this dislocation in human affairs, at least there can be no mistaking its character. What we are brought up against at every turn in the working of our present economic system is a restrictive veto on consumption; a veto so peremptory that under its compulsion we have had to labour to plough back again into the ground the crops we have laboured to produce; to burn supplies in vast quantities or dump them into the sea while armies of people are hungering for them. When the American administration, in compliance with this anti-consumer drive of the system, ordered the slaughter of millions of pigs and the burning of the carcases, there were crowds of American citizens —I myself have seen them so engaged—searching in garbage dumps for filthy scraps of nutriment, near enough to that great barbecue to have the reek of it in their nostrils. And in the background of this actual destruction of already produced supplies there is the steadily insistent general discouragement of production itself, under which a great part of the world's producing equipment is at any given moment standing idle, and aggregate output rarely gets beyond a meagre fraction of capacity. When simple discouragement does not exercise sufficient restraint upon production to satisfy the anti-consumer purposes of our economy, positive prohibitions are enforced. Quota allowances are imposed upon production, so that it becomes a criminal offence to produce beyond the prescribed allowance; to put into the market milk for want of which children by the thousand are suffering under-nourishment, or to grow the cotton urgently needed by vast armies of people who are without a spare shirt to their backs. In the last resort the prohibition becomes total, as when American farmers are subsidized for keeping their land out of cultivation.

This compulsion to go without things is imposed upon us all round; upon our public life and our social services as well as upon our private satisfactions. So far, indeed, from detecting and arresting the evil, the governing statesmanship of the world finds itself not only headed off at every turn from movement in the consumer direction, but positively driven, in any attempt it makes to cope with it, to do the very thing it sets out to prevent. The imperative of the system imposes itself upon the very effort to escape; compelling such effort to take the form of yet further insistence upon the anti-consumer view of human affairs; insistence that the world cannot afford to use its own visibly abundant real resources, and must go on economizing in every direction. The thing has a grip on the world's life like the ju-jitsu arm-breaking grip which utilizes the victim's own movement for release as an added leverage for making the fracture worse. The injunction drastically enforced everywhere—never because of any natural scarcity in our real resources, but in a world in which everything needful or desirable, everything servicable for the full satisfactions of human life, can be produced in greater plenty than any previous generation of men have known or dreamed of—is that we must cut down to the utmost our consumption of the things thus lavishly producible, and our carrying-on of the mutual services by which we might be enriching our common life almost illimitably.

In this way of living to which it subjects us, the economic system within which the world's affairs are now conducted reveals itself quite unmistakably as an anti-consumer system; not simply failing in a negative way to function for consumption, but actively and rigorously mandatory against it. Such universal and identical results are not mere accidents of mismanagement in a system capable of functioning for the consumer if well-managed. There is in all this something much more formidable than a chancey muddle into which incompetence has landed us. There is nothing haphazard about it. It is the working of a system in whose operations a set direction is visibly manifest and consistently followed; with a set purpose in it; a purpose clearly demonstrated, by the test of the results thus eventing from it in general human experience, to be at war with the consumer needs of mankind.

* * * * *

When, therefore, President Roosevelt, recognizing that making the interest of the consumer the directing purpose in economic procedure must be the determining policy in any New Deal which is to be effective, describes such a purpose as "a fundamental change in economic thought," he is not indulging in any rhetorical extravagance. He states a plain fact with sober precision. It is not merely change, but fundamental change; change in the very foundations of our economic life; change in the basic purpose to which economic procedure is directed.

My aim in this brief study is to set out, as simply as may be, what seem to me to be the implications in action and procedure of this fundamental change in economic thought and purpose.

For it is not enough that we see, however plainly, the getting of the world's real plenty to consumers as the final objective. That only states our problem for us. It does not solve it. It may be—and for very many people still is—nothing more than the instinctive recoil of the normal sane mind from what everybody feels to be the sheer unreason of human deprivations in the midst of ample power to satisfy human needs. That is all to the good as the beginning of real movement; for it is only from such deep instinctive feeling that the dynamic of any effective change can come. But that feeling has now become widely prevalent and is eager for guidance; a diffused resentment as yet unformulated for any effective action; astronomically nebulous, like those

> Vast tracts of glowing vapour not yet shaped
> Into the point and brightness of a star.

The immediate urgent practical need is a clear and purposeful understanding of what this consumer-economics concept implies in definite social structure and in economic procedure. And it is as a contribution towards such an understanding that this short study is intended.

## CHAPTER TWO

To get any such clear understanding with regard to procedure *for effecting fundamental change* is not easy. There are certain deeply-rooted mental habits and inertias which make the approach to such an understanding very difficult for most of us; and it is important at the outset that we should see clearly what is the character of this difficulty and how it operates to thwart the beginnings of any movement towards fundamental change.

What is demanded from us, for any valid judgment as to the procedure for effecting fundamental change, is a mental attitude wholly different from that in which the minor changes and adjustments, constantly needed to keep an existing economy going, have to be planned and executed. Even the most stable system of human life requires continuous minor internal adjustments of that sort. Assuming the essential purpose of an economy, its central principle of action, to remain unchanged, such running adjustments are effected by the ordinary familiar procedures of the system itself. And these procedures, by long force of habit and familiarity, come to be regarded by the mass of people as ways of carrying on human affairs quite independent of and unrelated to the central purpose of the system itself. They are taken to be the necessary natural procedures for carrying on human life in any circumstances; effective for making any change whatever, whether it be fundamental or only a minor change of adjustment within the existing system.

Thus, while it is quite easy for most people to see a large vague new purpose such as "serving the interest of the consumer" or "producing for use instead of for profit"; and quite easy to recognize in a general way, as Mr. Roosevelt does, that such concepts involve a fundamental change in the order of things; it is extraordinarily difficult for them to realize that the challenge of any change *which is really fundamental* is necessarily a challenge to all the familiar procedures by which the challenged established order is carried on.

It is this which accounts for the fact that action for dealing with the confusion into which life is thrown by our present deprivations in the midst of plenty, action taken even by the most well-intentioned Government, has been so generally futile. Worse than futile, indeed, since almost invariably it becomes a further insistence upon the deprivations and economizings. Seeking to implement a new vaguely seen consumer purpose by procedures *which are in fact the working apparatus of an anti-consumer economy*, naturally we get very little but disillusionment after disillusionment served up to us in the results.

We have to approach such a study, therefore, realizing that the implementing of a consumer purpose in our economy must of necessity involve very fundamental challenges to many things which, by reason of this mental inertia, the current thought of the times does not regard as being included in the challenge at all. Unless we come to our task with minds prepared for that necessity, we shall get nowhere; as indeed experience should have taught us by now. It is vitally important, therefore, that we should have some dependable test for throwing out procedures which are nothing but the working apparatus of an anti-consumer policy; procedures which would reduce to futility any attempt we might make to achieve our consumer purpose by their usage. That is what has happened to so many well-intentioned New Deal efforts, and what must always happen until we learn that our new and fundamentally changed purpose demands a new procedure fitted to its own requirements.

Nothing, I think, but a basic realism in our scrutiny of the problem will serve us for understanding in this matter; an insistence that all our thinking about the procedures shall be in terms of real things and real activities. My own rule in this research is a very simple one, but it does, I find, give guidance and direction through the labyrinth of illusions and confusions with which the mind of the world is beset in this task.

I try to anchor my mind to begin with on the basic fact that the only real happening in the economic life of mankind is the provision of actual goods and services for the satisfaction of human wants; and that nothing whatever enters or can enter into that reality other than *the natural resources of the world we live in and what human effort can make of them.* And having got an unshakable hold upon that, I do not allow any procedure or economic formula, any method of reckoning or of making accountancies, to get past my mind without telling me precisely what it stands for in relation to the real things and the real activities. I find that to be a pretty effective test; a sort of photo-electric eye for detecting illusions and throwing out counterfeits.

If we are to detect and correct the causes of the failure of our existing economy to make sense of life, let us apply this research test to its procedures. Let us apply it in the first place quite generally. Ask yourself this simple question: What is the basic real process by which human life is carried on? Simple as such a question looks, you will find it extraordinarily difficult, if you put it to the first hundred people you meet, to get them to reply to it *in realist terms.* The hypnotism which any traditionally established procedure for carrying on human affairs exercises over our minds is so tremendous that we take these procedure-devices to be the basic real processes. Born and bred and brought up in familiarity with them, most people take them for granted as outside the range of scrutiny or question, and accept them as natural laws of human living.

And so the mass of people cannot get beyond money procedure in answering such a question. The nearest they can get to realism—the farthest they can carry their minds down to fundamental things—is to the concept of human life being carried on by a process of buying and selling the things necessary for living.

But that, as a moment's reflection must tell us, is not a realist concept at all. The problem to be solved, on that concept of the essential process of human living, becomes a problem of how mankind may provide itself, not directly with real things, but with *purchasing power.* And when you begin to talk about purchasing power, you are already far away from any real starting-point, and in another region altogether from the region of basic realities. Purchasing power is a concept entirely within the framework of an established monetary system, which has to do, not with real things at all, but with the procedures of accountancy and the reckonings of value to which our permitted usage of the real things has become subject. We have to go deeper than that for our bedrock foundations and for the essential definition of our problem.

The bedrock realist fact in human economy is

the struggle of mankind with Nature for sustenance; and in the natural realism of that struggle the basic process by which human life is carried on is a process of *producing and using*.

Let us be quite clear on that. No physical reality whatever enters or can enter into our human economy other than this process of producing and using; human effort handling and shaping and moving natural resources through production into use. All monetary procedure belongs to the artificial framework of economic devices by which this real process of delivering goods into human use is made subject to certain reckonings and accountancies and valuations by which the central purpose of the economic system within which the money operates, and of which it is the accounting instrument, is made effective in our permitted usage of the real things.

It may, on examination, reveal itself to us as an excellent accounting device. But it also may not. On the facts actually eventing in human life from its operations, the presumption is rather against it. We may get light on that, however, as our inquiry develops. My point at this stage is that at any rate we cannot safely begin by taking anything for granted about it. Somewhere within this artificial framework of economic accountancy devices there lurks the irrationalism we are seeking to uncover; and if we begin by taking anything for granted about it, we shall run the risk of letting the very thing for which we are seeking—the secret of our present deprivations amid plenty—slip past us and escape scrutiny. Obviously we must compel all such procedure, including the concept of purchasing power and the procedure of buying and selling, to tell us exactly what it stands for in the movement of real things and services, and how it is related to the basic reality of life as a process of producing and using.

Into this natural realism of human life as a process of producing and using, our existing economy introduces a third term, thrust in between the producing and the using. And in doing so, it sets up an entirely altered concept of our basic necessary way of living. Fitting things into their operative sequence, what we are asked to accept as the basic natural procedure of living is a procedure of producing, *and then having to buy back what we have produced before we can use it.*

We must assuredly look at that rather closely. For on any sane presumption in the carrying on of human affairs, we *have* provided ourselves with what we need when we have produced the needed supplies. To what real fact in the natural physical sequence of living is this further requirement of "purchasing power" related?

It is in this middle term, this buying and selling interpolation between the producing and using of the natural sequence, that monetary procedure operates; and quite obviously it must be somewhere in the operation of this interpolated procedure that the failure of our existing economy to translate our real abundance into human satisfactions takes place. For if the realist producing and using process were in operation without interference, the world would—as a simple matter of two and two making four—be living up to its capacity for supplying itself with the things it needs; instead of being disabled, as in fact it now is, from using what it can produce; and even from producing up to more than a fraction of its productive capacity, because of the known inhibitions on getting the supplies, urgently needed though they are, into use if they were produced.

Carrying the analysis a step further, we find that this buying and selling is carried on by an accountancy procedure of costs and prices; costs which are accounted as being necessarily and naturally incurred in production, and must therefore be recovered in prices from the consumer. This "costs" accountancy takes us back to procedures and requirements in production itself; and would seem, therefore, to be the starting-point of the whole reckoning by which the process of buying and selling and ultimate price-recovery from the consumer is carried on.

It is, therefore, upon this concept of "costs of

production" that our scrutiny must first be concentrated. It is, I think we shall find, the basis of all the reckoning in our existing economy, the central concept on which the whole finance accountancy depends; and an understanding of it is the real master-key to an understanding of the failure of our existing economy to serve the consumer needs of the world's people.

## CHAPTER THREE

If you examine, by our realist test, anything which is accounted as a "cost of production," you will find, when you trace it down to the real movement of real things of which it purports to be an accounting, that it is never anything other than the use and consumption of already existing and usable things which goes on while further things for *future* use and consumption are being produced.

Stated as a generalization in that way, it is perhaps not so lucid, without further explanation, as one could wish. Let us try and make it clearer by looking at how it works out in particular cases.

You, let us say, are an employer with a thousand men engaged in your factories producing, well, any sort of manufactured article you like to imagine. You pay them wages; and the money you pay out in that way has to be entered in the accountancy of your business as a cost of producing the goods which will come to completion later on from the work your men are doing when they receive the wages.

That is the accountancy. But what are the actual happenings of which it is supposed to render an account? Let us look and see what in fact is the movement of goods effected by that payment of wages. Follow the money into its actual usage;

and you will find it functioning as purchasing power for the food and clothes and other satisfactions which the wage-receivers require *for their current sustenance.* To go back to our generalization, what this "cost of production" actually stands for is the use and consumption of already existing and usable things created and made available, not by the work which is being done at the moment, but by the past and completed productive energies of the community.

You have other costs besides wages; but if you will extend your scrutiny over all of them—if you extend it as widely as you will over the whole range of our economic life—everywhere and invariably you will find that the only real movement of real things effected by any "cost of production" disbursement of money is the movement into consumption and usage of the supplies and materials and implements made available for consumption and use by past production; the output of already completed human activities, to which output nothing has contributed other than the material resources of the world and what human effort has made of them.

We begin, do we not, by this realist test, to discover certain rather queer things about this accountancy of "costs of production." In the actual facts, this supposed cost of producing new goods turns out on scrutiny to have nothing whatever to do with production at all. It is a purely *distributive* process; and it is solely related—in the actual usage of the money so accounted and in the movement of real things which it effects—solely related to the distribution and use of already existing and usable things.

A still closer scrutiny will reveal the fact that it is not just one particular or exceptional form in which distribution takes place. It is the sole and only distributive process by which any supplies are allowed to get into use and consumption within our existing economy. The consumer or user must have "purchasing power"; and purchasing power is only allowed to reach him by passing the disbursement of it to him through this "costs of production" accountancy, and entering it up as a debt to be recovered in prices set up against the community's permitted usage of future goods when they in turn come to completion. You will search in vain over the whole field of our existing economy for any permitted possession of purchasing power by consumers against which this price-debt in regard to the usage of future supplies is not set up.

You see the sort of question which begins to confront us in all this. A debt to whom and on what ground? The community has already, by its own working effort applied to natural resources, created the actual supplies. Nothing else whatever, in the reality of things, has entered into their making. On what footing and by what entry does this new and mysterious indebtedness get into the accountancy?

Let us get the facts as to this as clear as possible. Under the hypnotism of this established procedure, the ordinary concept of how human life is sustained runs something like this: You, we will say, are working in production. But your current work does not come to fruition in a usable commodity until some time later; over most of the range of the world's activity, not until much later. The work now being done, for example, on the land in the late autumn season at which I am writing, will not result in the appearance of usable things until the harvest is gathered in a year hence. In the operations of power-production, when so much of the world's effort is devoted, not to the direct production of consumers' goods, but to preparing the apparatus and the powers for their production, the interval between current work and the appearance of goods usable by consumers may be and often is much longer than that.

But during the interval human life has to be maintained. It is accounted in our existing economy as being maintained by advances of credit—wages and other disbursements of purchasing power—against that future output. And the orthodox economic and finance assumption is that without incurring this indebtedness, by getting credit supplied to us through a finance accountancy, we could not live during the waiting period while the product of our current work is maturing.

When we turn to the facts and note what the physical reality, the actual happening, is, all this concept of "credit advances" is seen to be the most grotesque absurdity imaginable. We do *not* live upon the work we are now doing. All production is a new creative act; preparation for future usage and consumption; creative foresight for the requirement of years to come; the creative antithesis to any concept of cost. What we actually live on is the already reaped harvest of our past and completed work. And in the natural processes of human economy, our sole and only enablement to consume supplies—our sole natural authorization to consume them—is not the work we are now doing but the fact that we *have* produced them.

There is nothing in this concept of "credit" but sheer illusion. Its implications are so subtly and universally diffused through all the accountancy of our economy that, if you examine the established procedure at any point, you find everywhere in it the same assumption that the world lives, and can only live, on the consumability of next year's harvest advanced to us through a finance and monetary accountancy. And every such supposed advance of credit for the future fruition of our current work turns out on scrutiny to have no relation whatever in actual fact to the fruition of our current work; to be never in reality anything other than a permit to use and consume the completed output of our own past work.

Somewhere or other in the operation of this weird accountancy that output, obviously, has been barred against our direct right to use it—which should, in the ordinary sane sequence of things, follow naturally upon our having produced it—and made subject to this new requirement of "purchasing power" only issued to us as an indebtedness against which future output has to be mortgaged and in its turn barred out from direct consumption in the same way.

In relation to actual facts and to any possible physical reality, the whole notion of "credit" in this accountancy is the craziest absurdity. And it is just as wild an absurdity if you call it "social credit" or apply any other imaginable qualification to it. In no case does it represent anything that really exists or happens or can conceivably exist or happen. The absurdity is not simply some misuse of "credit" made by our existing economy, something that could be set right by using "credit" differently, calling it "social credit" instead of bankers' finance, and so on. It is the essential idea of "credit" itself which is the absurdity. It is pure myth. There is no such thing; no reality in the actual process of human living to which it corresponds in any way. Nothing ever is or ever can be advanced to us for usage or consumption in anticipation of its actual physical completion in production.

* * * * *

And now let us take the vital step from this technique of procedure to the human significance of it. Summing the whole thing up, you see that what the concept of "costs of production" actually stands for is nothing other than *the current sustenance of human life and human activity*. It is you and I, as human beings needing sustenance and things to use in our activities, who are the "costs." What our scrutiny begins to uncover is, therefore, something much deeper and more important than a technical point in accountancy. It is nothing less than a debased and extraordinarily grotesque concept of human life itself that emerges from all this; *a concept of it, not as the purpose which an economic system exists to serve, but as a burden which the economic system has to carry.*

And that is false accountancy. How profoundly false and how deadly in its implications in human life, I cannot find words adequate to convey. In any sane view of the vital relations between mankind and the fruits of human effort applied to the resources of the world, consumption—which is human living and sustainment and survival—is not a cost of the things we produce, but the end to which we produce them. And this reckoning of human life as a "cost"—

the reckoning on which all the procedure of our existing economy is based—does, I think, give us the real clue which we are seeking to the failure of the existing system to serve human needs or to make sense of life.

Consider it in relation to the perfectly sound distinction which is made in ordinary goods-production between intermediate and final products. The production of any consumable thing, any final product, goes back and back along many lines and through many stages of preparatory and equipment activity. One of the many preliminaries, for example, to the gathering in of a wheat crop is the manufacture of ploughing and drilling and harvesting machinery. Such machines have no purpose which stops short at themselves. They are intermediate products, whose only purpose is to enter into further products; and they are quite meaningless and purposeless except in relation to the further products. In their own form as machines the consumer has no direct use for them. They do not pass out to the consumer. They remain within the producing system; and as they become worn out in service there, they pass out to consumers in the wheat supplies into whose production they have entered.

But is the wheat itself when ripened and gathered any more a final product, the achievement of a final purpose in itself, than the tractor or the harvester was? Assuredly not. Just as the only function of the tractor was to disappear in the service of producing wheat, so in turn the only function of the wheat is to disappear in the service of producing the vigour and the survival of human life. *The only final product is human life.* And the final process by which alone production becomes complete is the consumption which transforms into human life all the raw material of goods-products preparatory to it.

Do not, I beg of you, take that as a figure of speech. It is the reality, and the only reality, of production; the single, central, substantial reality in human economy; the only thing that gives any sense or meaning to the production of material goods at all. Cut off from that completion, all the preceding and preparatory things become meaningless and unreal; and all the accumulation of goods-products up to that point a mass of dead, aborted, useless things which have stopped short of the only real purpose of production.

* * * * *

It is at this point that we come to close grips with the practical outcome of all this technical analysis. For that stopping short of the only real purpose in goods-production is precisely what happens in our existing economy.

And it does not happen by accident. To ensure

its happening is the central and essential purpose of our existing social order; and all the procedures we have been examining are the designed procedures for making that purpose effective. Turning our scrutiny, as we must now do, to the basic things in the established social structure, we shall find that all this finance accountancy, which is such unintelligible gibberish in relation to the physical realities of producing and using, is a perfectly accurate accounting in relation to the central governing purpose of the economic system within which it operates. It is an economic system which does not produce for use, but deliberately and of set purpose for the alienation from the mass of the world's people of the right to use and consume what they produce; and all its finance, its monetary reckoning of costs and prices and credits, is the account-keeping *of this alienation*, and not of a consumer purpose in production at all.

## CHAPTER FOUR

Every inquiry into economic procedure, if it is a real attempt to reach clear understanding, takes us straightway beyond the procedure to this essential question of what is the human purpose the procedure is designed to serve. If economic discussion, particularly in regard to money, is so often tediously unrevealing of anything of real importance, it is because it so often concerns itself only with the technique of the procedure, as if that were an end in itself, and detailed information about it the only purpose of economic study. Such mere knowledge of procedure technique, however extensive, has no significance of its own at all, and only becomes important in relation to the vital human purposes for whose effective expression *in actual human relationships* the procedures are designed.

A social structure is, *au fond,* not a set of institutions and procedures, but a set of human relationships of which the institutions and procedures are the vehicle. And if we are to arrive at any real understanding of our consumer problem—any real understanding of what making the consumer purpose the governing purpose in human economy means by way of the possible usage or non-usage of existing institutions and procedures for implementing it—it is upon that question we must concentrate. What are the essential human relationships which the existing social structure is designed to carry along and sustain? The human relationships which, in actual fact and practice, it does carry along and sustain?

At every stage in this inquiry we must keep our realist frame of reference continuously in mind. Let us here once again repeat it. It is:

> That the only physical reality in the economy of human living is in the natural resources of the world and what human effort can make of them;
>
> that this effort means an incessant struggle of mankind with nature for sustenance and satisfactions;
>
> that all economic systems and forms of social structure are the endeavours of mankind to organize and regulate that struggle as effectively as possible for the requirements of human living;
>
> and that the concept of how, and by what human relationships, the requirements of life may be best served, as that concept finds expression in economic systems and social structures, is always conditioned by the physical demands which the basic struggle with nature makes upon us and the physical possibilities within which it limits us.

What, then, are the actual facts of social structure, and of human relationships within it, which give form and definition to the existing economic system? It is to the clear definition of the facts, and not to any sort of opinionative argument about them, that we must first direct our attention; the essential framework facts, stripped as completely as we can get them stripped of non-essential and merely secondary detail.

This existing economic system is the organization and regulation of the human struggle with nature by the set-up of a social structure of which the basic condition is that the sources of the community's sustenance and its producing opportunities are privately owned. It is a property system. That is the bedrock foundation on which the whole structure rests.

And that, definitely and of necessity, makes the social structure a class structure, with two entirely different ways of living for its separate classes. Not merely different in degrees of wealth and standards of living, but different in the method by which the things required for living are obtained.

The property-owning class live by their proprietorship of the community's opportunities to produce, *such proprietorship carrying with it the right of property over all the produced output*; the class of non-owners, the working life of the world, being employed by such owners, and having no assigned or accredited claim on the resources of the community except by being so employed.

The essential and defining characteristic of the system is in this fact that within its operations all the produced output of supplies passes automatically, at its origins in production, into the property system. The working life of mankind does not, in producing supplies, produce any consuming rights over them for itself. Within the code of the system, the members of the working community can, in fact, be indicted for theft and robbery if they carry off an atom of their own product for their own direct use. All production within the system is the creation of property for the owners of the sources and the implements of its production.

It is *the entire output* which is thus appropriated into the property system. It is true that the working community gets its hire. But that, as we have seen in the previous analysis of costs and credit, is in no way related to the output of the world's current labours, and does not constitute anything in the nature of a property title over the goods to whose production the hired service is applied. It is simply an assignment to the working life of the world, from the store of supplies already completed in production and appropriated into the property system, of the sustenance without which the human adjunct to production could not be kept in operation. A cost to the property system in precisely the same accounting category as the fodder which has to be assigned to cattle for the same reason, or the fuelling of engines which also could not go on operating without it. Production within the property system is the production of property rights over *all* output; working costs and expenses, whether human or inanimate, notwithstanding.

* * * * *

The property system, in these essentials, has prevailed in the economy of human society for many ages. It has taken many forms: direct slavery, serfdom, many varieties of forced labour, and in our own time the hiring of nominally free men for wages. But its essential and defining characteristic—that all output produced within its set-up of economic relationships passes automatically into the property system—remains unchanged and unmodified.

When you owned slaves, for example, you owned all that the slaves produced. That was the essential purpose served by owning slaves; not the mere gratification of owning men, but the fact that such ownership carried with it the ownership of the product of their labour. And the economic relations set up by the existing property system work out to precisely the same end in regard to the product of nominally free men hired in modern industry; no man, of course, being really free within a system in which his access to all opportunities to live and work is barred against him by property rights over them. In effect, you own men when you own their essential means of life and work; and so, like the slave, they too produce, not consuming rights for themselves, but a property output for the owner of their opportunities to produce.

Within such a system, all sustenance assigned to the working life of mankind is quite correctly described as a "cost"; for all such sustenance is obviously the loss by the property system of such goods as have to be given up to provide the sustenance. The system, so far as the mass of mankind are concerned, stops short of the only real purpose in goods-production, the consumer purpose. In relation to the working life of the world, the production of wealth is taken to be completed with the delivery of the goods into the property system. Beyond that point, into the completion of the producing process by the use and consumption which carries the goods-production into human life itself as the final product, the hired workers of the world have no right to follow the goods, and would be merely trespassers breaking into the property domain to steal what is not theirs to use and consume.

In the physical facts of life, however, the gap thus created between the production of goods and their use and consumption by the working life of the world, cannot be left entirely unbridged. The physical facts make it necessary, since the production of goods cannot be kept going unless a sufficient supply of labour is kept alive in working fitness, that a certain amount of sustenance must be passed on to the working life of the world as an unavoidable cost. For the time being, at any rate, that cost is unavoidable; until such good time as the complete robot becomes available which will be capable of performing all the work of goods-production without the costly human drawback of having to be fed while doing it.

But the human life thus sustained is not accounted in this property economy as the purpose of production at all, nor regarded as itself being the ultimate wealth for which all the goods-production is preparatory. The whole accountancy of costs and prices and credit is the accountancy by which, in accordance with the governing purpose of the property system, human life is struck out of the reckoning in that character, and is entered up instead as a burden the property system has to carry, a drain on its resources, a cost to which the rule of the system about costs—that they must be kept down to the lowest possible point—must be rigorously applied.

See also how accurately the "advance of credit" accountancy fits in. Mere impossible nonsense as it is in relation to the realities of producing and using and the physical facts of life, it is really quite simple and accurate as an accountancy adjusted to the purpose of making the property title to all produced output appear in the final reckoning.

The accountancy on this point is well worth while following closely in detail right through; for it is a most skilful and ingenious piece of legerdemain with figures, and highly entertaining for the bland way in which it turns all the realities involved in the matter upside down and presents them in complete reversal for our acceptance as accounted facts.

It begins by accounting money (which can in fact only function for getting existing goods into distributed use) as being issued to finance further production; and in that way credits itself with having advanced the consumability of next year's harvest to us for current consumption. It then goes on, by accounting that current consumption as costs against the next harvest, to debit us with having eaten it all up before the harvest itself comes into physical existence; so that when in the end the harvest is actually reaped we are accounted as owing it to the property system in repayment of the advance. An accountancy by which the passing of all the output of the world's work into the property system in an endless serial gets entered into the reckoning, not as the direct seizure which in fact it is, but as a payment due to the property system for value received by the working producers! The value received being the assignment to them, from the harvest which the property system had already seized away from them, of the sustenance physically necessary to enable them to produce another harvest for similar seizure.

When you attempt thus to relate the finance

procedure to the physical realities and the actual movement of goods, the accountancy, as you see, turns out to be the most unintelligible nonsense imaginable. But in relation to the property purpose, it is a quite sound and effective reckoning. Its sole concern is to register and maintain property title-deeds over the output of the world's producing activities, and to eliminate accordingly from the reckoning any entry of the working life of the world as authorized possessor of that output by title of having produced it.

To bring the property title into the reckoning in that way is what the finance of a property system exists for. In any accountancy of a physical utility and consumer purpose in production, it would of course be the craziest nonsense to enter up any real thing as being advanced into use and consumption before it exists. But when production is carried on, not as the creation of physical utilities for the consumer, but of property rights for the owner, the reckoning has to be a reckoning of the property rights, and not of the physical utility character of products in relation to a consumer purpose; and the accountancy registration of the property claims at the stage when they actually arise, at the origin of goods in the activities of production and by imminent right of ownership of the means of producing them, is perfectly accurate accounting.

If the accountancy makes nonsense of the physical

realities, that is only because it is the accountancy of an economic system which makes nonsense of human affairs by imposing deprivations in the midst of abundance upon the mass of humankind. If the barrier between human life and the available abundance producible from natural resources were a visible physical barrier, it would assuredly be torn down promptly enough. But our available resources —"within easy reach," as Mr. Roosevelt so truly says—are not denied to us by any such obvious process of seizure and restraint. There is no obvious seizure. The resources are not taken from us; they never get to us. The property system is not a procedure for diverting supplies from us when we have possessively produced them. It is *the process of production itself* which is carried on as a property process. The supplies make their original appearance inside the property enclosure, where the process by which they are seized is protected against any real scrutiny by the hypnotism which traditionally established basic institutions exercise over men's minds.

That hypnotism, although it is now manifestly, and happily, weakening as against the counter-impact of real experiences upon the world's thinking, is still strong enough to prevent large numbers of people, when they find themselves up against deprivations in the midst of plenty, from raising the fundamental question of why the supplies come into existence thus alienated from our usage; barred in a property enclosure to begin with against the consumer needs of the community. The only question which, under this hypnotic influence, they imagine can be raised is whether, and how, we can get ourselves supplied with purchasing power for redeeming our products from the property enclosure a little more commensurately with our consumer needs; whether, and how, the property system can safely incur and carry the enlarged cost of parting with its property—the supplies it appropriates in production—on a somewhat larger scale of permitted current consumption by the community.

All such permitted current consumption within the property system has to be computed by the essential property reckoning; the consumption must always and necessarily be charged up as a cost against further production and must be recovered in prices from the consumer. So that whatever additional purchasing power the community gets with which to redeem goods from the property enclosure for use is automatically added to the price charge which the property system levies upon the community when the goods are issued. The cost and the price are not two separate things, but the double entry of the same thing on the two sides of the reckoning, the "cost-price" which is the minimum the property system *must* recover from the consumer if it is to remain in existence as a property system. To compute the permitted consumption of the community in any other way would be to strike the property rights out of the reckoning as the effective title to possession and set up the consumer needs of the community instead.

That, of course, is what a production-for-use economy would do. It would be the procedure naturally fitted to its consumer purpose in production. But it cannot be done within the property economy, whose purpose in production is the creation of the property title over all output; for you cannot destroy a title and retain it at the same time.

The accountancy of all consumption as a cost recoverable in prices is essential so long as the property procedure in production itself remains. And since these property computations of costs and prices and credits and the financing of production are still accepted in general thought as the basic necessary natural computations in human affairs, when the final account, working out as it invariably does at a life of deprivations for the mass of mankind in the midst of plenty, is rendered to us in terms of these computations, and the mere mechanical adding-up and subtraction proves to be correctly performed, we pass it without any real questioning, and accept as financial necessity deprivations which we know to be natural absurdities.

The idea that these computations, which are

nothing whatever but the accountancy of the essential anti-consumer purpose of the existing property system, can be so manipulated as to *finance consumption* within the property system is inherently absurd. No social economy into whose reckoning costs and prices and credits enter can have a consumer purpose; for costs and prices are never anything other than measurements of the obstacles which a property economy puts up against consumers. The essential fallacy of the various money-manipulating schemes for issuing social-dividend claims upon the output of the world's industry, not to the owners of the industry, but to the general consumer public, is in the assumption that a consumer distribution can be effected by a distribution of *money* while *the goods themselves* continue to be produced as property alienated from the community to begin with. The two things are incompatible; so far as the direct consumer claims are asserted, the property title is cancelled.

All such schemes, as well as the more orthodox attempts of New Deal Governments to get sustenance goods over to the mass of resourceless people with whose human needs Governments everywhere are now confronted, accept the property procedure *in production itself* as the basis of our economic life; and fail to see that it is there that the alienation of supplies from the community is effected. Their effort at money-manipulation only begins after the mischief is done and the maldistribution for which they are seeking a remedy has been effectively achieved. They approach the whole thing, not as a problem of producing butter for consumption to begin with, but as a problem of retrieving the butter from the dog's mouth after the dog has got away with it; and indeed on the assumption that he must not be interfered with in getting away with it.

They see their problem, therefore, in an unreal and fallacious way; as a problem of finance instead of real things; of figures in accountancy and not actual goods in being; a problem, not of getting real things to consumers, but of distributing purchasing power; of buying and selling instead of producing and using; ignoring the vital fact that all this procedure of purchasing power and finance is itself nothing whatever but the intrusion of the property rights between the goods which the community has produced and the community's consuming rights over them.

If we see our consumer problem as a problem of finance, of purchasing power instead of production for use, we shall see it falsely. Throughout the whole business finance has nothing whatever to do with the intrinsic realities of production. All the money values are property values; reckonings and measurements of the property claim over real things against the consumer. They have no existence whatever except as figures and computations of the property titles. They represent nothing in the realities of materials or powers or production-efficiency; nothing whatever in the working capacity of the world's people to use the powers and shape the materials to human needs. These realities are in the physical facts of life, and in the accumulated racial knowledge with which we set about our task of drawing upon the physical resources of the world for the uses of human life; *and they are the complete and self-sufficient equipment of mankind for a production-for-use economy*. To a community possessing its own natural resources and planning its activities for the direct service of its own life, the whole monetary procedure would be meaningless, and the distribution of supplies to consumers a completely physical and non-financial process of putting the real things into the reach of those who need them; that being the sole purpose for producing them at all.

* * * * *

Charles Dickens, in *Bleak House*, referring to the common belief that the law is a maze of incomprehensible procedures with no definite purpose of social justice in it, remarks that it is really a very direct, simple and logical thing once you see what its real purpose is. If you begin by assuming that its purpose is to ensure justice to everybody, it must indeed seem to be a maze of tortuous practices which do not lead to any such result. But once you get hold of the fact that that is not what it exists for at all; that its real purpose is to make business for itself; how simple and direct and effective it is seen to be!

Well, the monetary system is rather like that. If it seems to you to be a labyrinth of meaningless procedures leading to no rational end, that is only because you have not observed what its real purpose is. If you begin by assuming that its purpose is to assist in getting goods distributed into use, then it must seem to be the most ineffective thing imaginable; for so far from getting goods distributed it leaves the mass of people disabled from using and consuming goods in the midst of copious abundance, and even destroys goods wholesale (for price reasons) rather than permit the people who need them to use them. But get hold of the fact that money is simply the working apparatus of a social economy whose basic purpose is to pass all goods into the property system at their origins in production; and that its sole business, in all its accountancy of costs and credits and prices, is not at all to distribute that property into general use, but to ensure that *no goods shall be permitted to escape from the property system into use without rendering up in prices the satisfaction of the property claim over them*; get hold of that essential function of money as a measure of property claims and an accountancy for ensuring their collection, and the whole thing becomes plain, simple, direct; and—as our consumer disablement in the midst of abundance testifies—thoroughly effective.

## CHAPTER FIVE

It must, however, be noted that, although the hypnotism which long-established and familiar institutions exercise over men's minds may account for their survival after urgent need has arisen for getting rid of them, it does not account for their establishment and their long period of unquestioned authority.

Devastatingly final as the evidence of the facts is in regard to the failure, and the congenital unfitness, of this property economy to serve the consumer needs of the world to-day, it is a system which has endured for many ages as the established structure of human society. And no structure of social organization could so survive and maintain itself in long stability unless it served, in some quite essential way, the requirements of human life in carrying on the struggle with nature for the satisfaction of human wants and cravings.

It was stable over immemorial generations; and that very stability is in itself, to anyone with a perception of the movement of history, convincing proof of some fitting and necessary purpose served by it in the natural history of human development. A social structure which has endured as the property system has endured must have its historic justifications in relation to the requirements of human life.

. . . Why, then, its sudden collapse in our time into these present world-wide confusions?

There can be no question as to the fundamental character of the indictment which the present facts of human experience prove against it. Not merely failure in management but congenital inability; a central governing purpose in it which works out in human life everywhere to-day as a general disablement of the community from using what it can readily produce; a central purpose inconsistent with the essential consumer purpose in production. The facts are beyond any controversy, both as to the character of the indictment and the completeness of the proof.

Current thinking may for a time be bewildered, as it now is, about *procedure*, but none the less the normal sane mind instinctively rejects the idea of any other *purpose* than a production-for-use purpose in our producing activities. The notion of a world devoting its resources and energies to any other end than serving human needs does not make sense, and cannot be fitted into any rational concept of life at all. The difficulty for most people is that they cannot even suspect the presence of the anti-consumer purpose in the familiar institutions and procedures which custom has led them to accept as the normal natural ways of living; and will not begin to look for it there until the deprivations which the collapsing structure inflicts upon them become so grave as to leave them no alternative. When, however, as in our scrutiny of the "costs of production" idea, we do begin to look at the present results of these familiar procedures with minds fixed realistically upon the natural facts and the actual requirements of mankind as *the only valid determinants of economic policy*, it is precisely that irrationality of an anti-consumer purpose in them which leaps out at us. Quite obviously the essential purpose of an economic system which thus reckons the satisfactions of human life as a burden of expense inflicted upon it, *must* be a purpose other than providing those satisfactions. And it is in strictest conformity with such reckoning that the system should, as in fact it does, work out in practice everywhere as a general disablement of the world's people from using and consuming the things they need urgently, and can produce plentifully.

The challenge thus raised by any real proposal to make the consumer purpose dominant in human economy goes, therefore, to the very foundations of the existing social structure. It is a challenge to the central principle of action of the property economy; and the conflict in which the raising of that challenge involves us is a conflict as to the basic purpose for which human activities are carried on, the basic purpose of production itself in relation to human life.

The system thus challenged is, as we know, a

system with long historic justifications, stabilized as the way of human living over practically all our past history; a stabilization unthinkable and impossible except in relation to a real service of the requirements of human life. Why, then, to repeat our question, why this sudden collapse into a world-wide confusion in human affairs?

The realist frame of reference which we have set up for this inquiry gives us the direction in which the answer to that question must be sought. "The concept of how, and by what human relationships, the requirements of life may be best served, as that concept finds expression in economic systems and social structures, is always conditioned by the physical demands which the basic struggle with nature makes upon us and the physical possibilities within which it limits us."

When, therefore, a long-established stable economy becomes unstable with a growing confusion of insecurity everywhere within the range of its operations, inflicting general disablements upon human life instead of serving human requirements, and is itself unchanged in the essential human relationships and class cleavages which are its necessary set-up in social structure, what we must expect to find is that the physical realities by which all our economic activities are conditioned have been so altered as to make the unchanged old economic procedures incompatible with the new facts.

And that is precisely what has happened. The conditions of the basic human struggle with nature have been revolutionized. The physical realities of production, the activities by which man wins his sustenance from nature, have taken a new character, fundamentally different from anything in previous human history. And our property economy, adjusted in all its procedures to the old physical determinants of human economy, is congenitally incapable of dealing with the new facts.

If, therefore, we are to get our question answered convincingly to reason—if we are to get a clear view of the magnitude and the character of the crisis to which the property economy of human living has come, and of the breakdown with which human civilization is menaced if we still persist in running our economy on the old lines—it is necessary to stand back from the detail for a little, and look at the thing as a whole in its relation to the fundamental change which has taken place in the mode of human living with the coming of power-production.

## CHAPTER SIX

If we think of the coming of power-production merely as a development of the technique of the world's work, we shall not even begin to understand its vital significance in the economy of human living. It is a superbly greater thing than progress in technique. It is a basic change in the character of the human struggle with nature for sustenance; not merely a new method of working, but a new kind of life for mankind, in which the "work" obligation which the carrying on of that struggle has up till now imposed upon us has been transformed into something completely different.

At every stage in such a study as this, we must keep on reminding ourselves that the only reality in the economy of human living is in natural resources and what human effort can make of them. But what human effort can make of natural resources is not a fixed quantity. It depends upon the knowledge man has of natural resources and their potentialities; and for long ages he had no knowledge at all of what was concealed below the exposed surface of things. Of metals, of the chemistry of things, he knew next to nothing beyond what lay on the surface for common observation. And of power other than his own physical exertions, power that, once he mastered its secret, he could evoke and control, compelling Nature herself to work for him instead of being merely a quarry of materials which he must work upon for himself, he had no real or effective knowledge at all.

In all the ages down to our own, what human effort could make of natural resources was conditioned by the fact that the energy at man's disposal for productive effort, the measure and the limit of the output he could win from Nature, was his own physical toil. His knowledge of material resources had been slowly expanding through the ages; but the dynamic resources remained hidden from him. He became extraordinarily ingenious in devising tools and mechanical appliances; but they were tools and appliances which were energized and kept in operation by his own bodily exertions. The productive output of a world of man-power was always meagre. It was a world of scarcity and of persistent demand for human drudgery to provide even that scarcity.

Power-production has swept that restriction and all its implications out of the way of human development. We have discovered that the natural resources from which our sustenance comes include, not only the materials which have to be shaped to our needs, but also the powers which can do the shaping with an effectiveness, and on a scale immeasurably greater, than we could ever do it for ourselves. We have called up, from their long concealment in the natural resources themselves, new gigantic, tireless, non-human physical forces to take the place of our own physical toil as the energy of production and the measure of output.

And with that the whole relationship of mankind to the struggle with Nature for livelihood has been fundamentally altered. It is not merely an extension of the old kind of knowledge we possessed about the resources at our disposal; not merely that we find Nature a richer quarry than before of materials on which to expend our toil. It is the entry of mankind into *a new realm of knowledge*; the discovery of a new world in which the whole economy of human living is on a new footing. The basic conditioning of all our activities—the compulsion we can apply to Nature to yield up to us what we need for living—has been changed, not simply in measure, but in essential character. It is no longer what our own meagre physical effort can secure for us, but what we can command Nature's own automatism of energies to serve up to us.

The abundance now available for human life is a new thing in the history of mankind. But we shall miss the significance of it if we think of the problem of this age as if the transition from scarcity to abundance were the governing factor in it. That is not the dynamic factor at all. The operative and defining factor in the change which has taken place in the world's life is not the abundance, but the new service by which we get the abundance; the displacement of human toil by non-human energies in production.

In all the ages down to our own, all social structures and devices, all our human artifices and methods of organizing our activities, have been the strategies and tactics of a struggle with nature carried on by human physical toil. Down to the last iota of social and economic organization, the determining factor in every system of human economy has been this basic dependence of the whole structure of life upon human drudgery. In all its procedures—in laws and customs and the motivization of conduct, in the compulsions imposed and the incentives provided—the carrying on of community life has had to be kept adjusted to this basic requirement of direct and continuous human toil for keeping the sustenance of the community going.

The man of only a few generations ago, if he could have borrowed Mr. Wells's "Time Machine," might have travelled back through immemorial generations without getting away from the essential structure and social aspect of his own familiar world. A peasant and handicraft world, with its human life widely scattered about in small self-contained village communities; a world without effective transport or communications, in which every district had to provide the main staple all-round needs of life for itself from local resources. . . . A world of scarcity and meagre living; meagre not only in its restriction to local supplies, but in the output of the hour of human drudgery which was its unit of productive energy. A world of scanty supplies laboriously wrung from natural resources; the condition of any achieved success in that stubborn struggle for existence being man's own unremitting physical effort.

It was in relation to, and as the working instrument of, that mode of human existence that the property system came into being, and remained stable so long as the conditioning of human life remained limited in that way. It was the attempt—on the whole the successful attempt—of human civilization, with its innate thrust towards things in life other than drudgery, to handle these natural conditions of scarcity and drudgery so as to get some sort of cultural life out of them.

While our only means of winning sustenance from Nature was unceasing human drudgery, no release of the general human life from that drudgery into cultural leisure was possible. But there was a possible way out for a favoured few, self-selected by the operation of the primitive rule that they should take who have the power and the cunning to enslave their fellows. For even under quite primitive conditions, Nature is sufficiently responsive to human physical efforts to enable the physical labour of a man to produce something beyond his own bare physical sustenance. With the establishment of property rights over natural resources—to which there is no possible original title whatever other than seizure by violence or by cunning—and the command over the labour of a community which follows from such ownership of their opportunities to live and work, it was possible to ration the drudge's permitted sustenance down to as low a level as would keep him fit for continuous working; and the lord of a community of drudges, taking from each the surplus beyond that permitted sustenance, could be released from the common obligation of drudgery into a life of cultural opportunity.

No other than such a restricted class release was possible in an economy of scarcity based upon human drudgery. The natural compulsions of an age of scarcity dependent upon human physical effort made it imperative, if the physical basis of life for the community was to be kept going, that the mass of the world's people should remain drudges. The property system was the device of the world's age of scarcity for effecting this limited class release. It arose under conditions of scarcity, and was related solely to the compulsions imposed upon mankind by those conditions; and in spite of the crudities of oppression to which class power over the lives of other men always gives rise, it did undoubtedly serve a real purpose in cultural human development as the only then available means of fostering it.

Power-production has made all these conditions of drudgery and scarcity obsolete in the process of winning human sustenance from Nature. It has given us slaves other than human to do our drudgery for us; and with their appearance human services are ceasing to be required as the physical energy of production and have become practically obsolete as the measure of output. It is by these new gigantic non-human energies that the world's natural resources are now wrought into products; with human service, over a constantly widening range of the world's production, only required for supervision and attendance upon them; and even that in a steadily diminishing degree, the supervision and attendance itself becoming every day more and more the automatism of the non-human natural energies themselves, as our technique for releasing and setting them to work becomes more and more developed. And the productive energy of these new slaves is so gigantic that for every hour of human time required in attendance on them we get an output of the things we need anything up to a thousand times greater than the hour of human time spent in the direct drudgery of action as the physical energy of production could ever win for us.

What is implicit in all this is the release of the general life of mankind into cultural leisure endowed with the full opportunities of which the new abundance is the measure. The old unhappy class breach in human life has become meaningless. It never, in fact, had any meaning or purpose other than as an endowment of cultural leisure for the few in a world whose possible output was so scanty, and obtainable only by such methods, as to make drudgery imperative for the mass of men. It is not incidentally, nor by some accident or mismanagement, nor in unessential or remediable detail, that the property system fails to set our new plenty flowing into the lifestream of the world. Its anti-consumer policy, its insistence upon economizing and restricting the use of our now ample resources, its universal poverty-amid-plenty consequences in the world's way of living, are in its fundamental character and purpose. They are the essential compulsions it exists to enforce upon the general community; the purposes implicit in its origins; the very design of its existence as a social structure.

It can work to no other ends. It came into being to meet the requirements of a period when the problem of human economy was how, from the hard conditions of life in a man-power age of drudgery and scarcity, to squeeze a provision by which cultural aspirations that were stifled in a life of drudgery might be endowed and given opportunity to develop. It was not set up by any planning or design, but by the urge in human civilization to these ends; seizing roughly and crudely upon the only available procedure for keeping the necessary drudgery going, and safeguarding the scanty output from being used up by the class relegated to that servitude.

The property system remains to-day unchanged in these essentials and purposes. The attempt to perpetuate the old man-power and scarcity-age device of social organization in this new world of a general release of human life from the conditions of drudgery and scarcity—the new world whose problem of human economy is how to live up to the leisure and the abundance which are implicit and unavoidable in the operation of the new producing forces—is no longer possible without bringing all civilization to catastrophe.

## CHAPTER SEVEN

THE conclusion to which such a general survey leads is clear and unmistakable. It is that our existing capitalist property system is a form of economic organization wholly incompatible with the new leisure and abundance consequences in human life which are implicit in the new powers in production; a system which is not simply incapable of providing, but in its intrinsic purposes and character is the direct negation of, any effective service of the new powers to the life of mankind. Not incapable merely by mismanagement or avoidable errors in administration, but by congenital and insuperable difference of natural function and *raison d'être*.

The validity of a conclusion so far-reaching, and so vital in its bearing upon the action necessary for dealing effectively with our existing economic confusions, must be tested in every aspect by the closest critical scrutiny we can bring to bear upon it. As we have seen, the hypnotism of any long-established system makes the mind of the average man very unreceptive to any idea of fundamental change in social structure. The general disposition is to go on trying out every imaginable expedient of patchwork reform within the existing order. But when, as is now the case, a decade in which that sort of effort, in every variety of reformist New

Deal ingenuity, has taken us up one blind alley after another without finding a way out, and left the world more perplexed than ever under disillusionment after disillusionment, a much more alert readiness to face up to the fundamental issue is manifesting itself. More and more clearly the inquiry concentrates on the real question: is the system itself capable of adjustment to the new conditions?

It is the essentially realist character of the evidence for fundamental change—evidence steadily confirmed by the unvarying failure of every merely reformist effort—that is now making the general mind more and more receptive to such a question. The average man has had certain justifications for shying off from suggestions of fundamental change in social structure; for such suggestions have often enough taken the form of idealist projects unrelated to facts or to the course of history; fanciful Utopian visions of how an imaginary ideal society of perfectly just men might be supposed to carry on its affairs. And while such visions may be very helpful and stimulating in the long-time process of the development of human character, the perfectly sound instinct of the average man is to brush them aside impatiently when they are offered to him as working projects in relation to existing institutions and the current needs of the day's work.

The present discussion is outside that field of

romanticism altogether. It has to do wholly with current facts and realities and their impact upon the needs of the day's work. The necessity for fundamental change in our economic life is a necessity arising, not from any fanciful conception of what the needs of life would be in another and a better world, but from the imperative of the new facts and conditions now actually established and operative in our lives.

The real fundamental change *has in fact already happened*. We are not at the beginning of a revolution. Our problem is that of handling the present and immediately pressing consequences in the current life of mankind of the revolution which *has* taken place. It is the accomplished fact that presents itself to us in all these current urgencies; insisting that we bring our economic procedures into working accord with the revolutionized conditions into which our life has been carried.

It is the existing economic structure itself which, essentially unchanged in a world of essentially changed physical actualities, has been left fantastically disconnected from the realities of producing and using. A sort of inverted Utopia; not projecting a dream future for us, as right-minded Utopias do, but insisting that we go on living in the old nightmare of the departed ages of scarcity and drudgery.

And since, unlike the pleasanter Utopianisms, it is not an unmaterialized dream of the future without any substance in affairs as medium through which to act upon our doings either for good or evil, but a survival in operation of actual forms and institutions from the past, it has the power of inflicting the mad compulsions of its nightmare upon our lives. Its continuance is nothing less than the abdication of human reason from the control of human affairs. What other possible interpretation will any sane future generation of men be able to put upon a period in history when—to cite but a single index-fact to its mentality—armies of children are habituated to under-nourishment while food-crops are burnt, dumped into the sea, or ploughed back into the ground, and the production of supplies kept under constant restriction *in fear of the price-consequences to the system of letting plenty get into its markets*?

*     *     *     *     *

The general survey we have been making sets up, unmistakably enough, a presumption amounting to practical certainty that this existing class structure of economic relationships based on property rights over the sources of wealth, and by sequel to that over all produced supplies, is incompatible with the new physical processes established in production itself; a presumption so strong that one might be tempted to leave it at that as a completed case.

But such a challenge to the fundamental things

which are rooted in the immemorial traditions of human economy cannot be left with any faintest suspicion of presumption in it. We must have nothing less than assured certainty about such a conclusion; and it is necessary to test its validity against a more finally definite and explicit scrutiny of the facts than a general survey can give us. We must go on to examine with a still greater precision what the new physical processes are, and what is their realist impact upon the old economic procedures by which we are still attempting to conduct our affairs.

The test must be wholly realist. It is on the evidence of the facts and the facts alone that judgment must rest. Whatever these actual changes which have taken place in the physical realities of production may be, it is obvious that no prolonged refusal to adjust our procedures to them is possible without disaster. They are the imperatives to which we must in the end adapt ourselves or be broken. It is just as well to remember that there is that alternative. It is not quite true to say that as between King Canute telling the tide to stop and the tide telling King Canute to move, the final word of authority is always with the tide. There is the possible alternative that King Canute may be stupid enough to prefer drowning to moving. And in view of the present condition of human affairs, with property-system Governments equipping themselves everywhere for wars of annihilation arising out of the economic rivalries of the system, and with an increasing percentage of people committing suicide as the easiest way out of their finance and employment worries, the possibility of human civilization persisting in that choice is certainly not one that can be lightly ruled out.

The three great changes made in the physical basis of human economy by the coming of power production are:

(1) Human labour has been superseded as the physical energy of production by non-human dynamic energies discovered in the natural resources of the world and brought under control for human service.

(2) Production, which was largely individual when human service functioned as the physical energy required for it, has become almost entirely communal by the new power-processes; from which usable things only pass out to consumers through a vast network of preparatory and equipment operations, and with world-wide activities so indistinguishably merged into them that no allocation of productive responsibility for the final product to individuals, or even to separate power-plant groups of individuals, is possible.

(3) Human labour, in ceasing to function as the

physical energy of production, has also ceased to be the measure of output. We get the output by the measure of the new powers; and their producing capacity, computed in output obtainable from them per hour of human time spent in setting them to work and attending to all their requirements, is so vastly greater than that of the hour of our own man-power that it has transformed our economy from an economy of scarcity to an economy of almost incredible abundance.

These are the new physical realities of the world's producing economy; the new conditioning of the processes by which the life of mankind obtains sustenance and satisfactions from the natural resources of the world; facts to which our human artifices of economic procedure have to be adapted. What is their impact upon the property-system class structure devised for coping with the difficulties of a man-power age of scarcity?

If we are to have clearly in mind the complete frame of reference for making our scrutiny effective at this point, we must again set out, not only what the new realities are, but with the same explicit definiteness what are the essentials of the economic organization whose capacity for dealing with the new conditions is the vital issue we are examining.

The property-system organization of our economic life is a class structure within which:

(1) The sources of the community's wealth are privately owned, and all produced outputs pass by automatic property right into the possession of the class owning the sources and implements of their production;

and (2) the working life of the world occupies a hireling status in relation to this ownership. Its only accredited footing in the system is its employment by the owners, and the only claim assigned to it for participation in the sustenance resources of the community is by being so employed.

These are the essentials of the property system; the points upon which it cannot be changed without ceasing to be a property system. The class relationship of master and hireling is not merely a matter of convenience to it. It is fundamental. Given the basic fact of private ownership over the community's sources of supplies, and these class assignments of status and functions and accredited rights are only its automatic expression in social structure and human relationships. If the property system is to remain a reality of actual hold upon the world's resources—and it ceases to be a property system if it does not—the non-propertied mass of mankind can have no footing for existence except as a source of service or profit to the owner class.

Let us, to begin with, leave out of consideration

for the moment any aspect of these facts which involves the passing of a moral judgment on the system; as to its justice or injustice, or the disparities it creates in human life, or the harsh oppression for which it gives opportunity. All that has nothing whatever to do with the essential question which must first be answered; the wholly practical question of fact. Can this property system, on the evidence of its own essential procedures, stand up to the new facts or work under the new conditions? The injustice and oppression of the system is written plainly enough in the history of all the ages of class servitude. *But it worked.* It maintained itself without breakdown or any serious menace of breakdown as the established procedure for carrying on the economy of human living, so long as the basic realist conditions of human life were man-power in production and scarcity in output. To those conditions its essential procedures were fitted. Can they be applied to the new economy of human living in which these basic realist conditions are completely reversed, and have become conditions of non-human physical energy in production and abundance in output?

Most questions of fact answer themselves when the facts are seen clearly. This one certainly does.

The property system, in its essential procedure, can make no provision for the regular sustenance of a non-propertied class except that they should be employed in the service of the owning class. Any other power to take sustenance from the resources of the community exercisable by a non-propertied class would clash with the property rights over the supplies so taken, and is impossible within a property economy, since it would be in direct and destructive contravention of the basic nature of the system.

The property system may—and since the owning class is not a class in the abstract, but a group of human beings amenable, within limits, to human sentiment, very often does—make *ex gratia* or charitable provision for sustenance when the system creates hard cases of resourcelessness calling for relief; but that does not in the least affect the basic status or the assigned function of the non-propertied working life of the world in a property economy; any more than sending out an ambulance to the men who are wounded in battle stops the war or alters its character as an activity expressly intended to inflict the wounds on them.

Such a social structure, within which no provision of power over sustenance other than by service rendered to ownership is possible for the mass of mankind, can therefore only be regarded as a possible permanent structure on the assumption that the services of the non-propertied man will always be continuously and regularly required by ownership. Otherwise, the mass of men, in the degree in which ownership ceases to require their service, are left with no accredited right to live at all.

The assumption that there must be such a continuous requirement for the services of the disinherited mass of the people was a quite valid assumption to make in the age of man-power in production. It accorded with the physical reality of production as a man-power process yielding a scanty output, and therefore demanding the utilization of the available labour to the full. If the property estate set up over the sources of the community's sustenance was to be fructified, this was the only energy available for doing it.

So far as the consuming needs of its servitors were concerned, the system was of course stringently anti-consumer; for then as now its essential purpose was to secure from their labour a greater yield in products than it need render back to them in sustenance. But although it kept them poor—"kept costs down" to use the modern finance euphonism for debarring the working life of the world from using and consuming more than a sustenance ration of its own products—it did at least utilize their services; and the physical realities of the man-power process of production justified it in the assumption that leaving them solely dependent upon being employed was a sufficient guarantee that at least a servitor's scale of sustenance would always be available for them.

Here, clearly and beyond all controversy, is a vital disconnection between the essential purposes and procedures of the property system and the essential character of the new realities in production.

With the coming of power production, the old assumption that the requisite sustenance of the disinherited class in a property economy is assured by the essential need of the owning class for their services—the assumption without which the property system becomes impracticable as a device for sustaining the life of a community—has ceased to have any validity at all. The operative function of the new powers, their essential and defining impact upon the human economy, is that they wipe out this only claim to live—the claim to be utilized in employment—which the property system gives, or can give, to any non-propertied class.

The basic fact in the revolution through which our producing economy has passed is this substitution of physical energies drawn from natural resources for man-power in production and service. Ownership, under the new conditions, gets its property estate in the sources of the community's supplies fructified more and more by the self-contained non-human productive energies of the estate itself, and with a constantly increasing automatism.

The technique of power usage is still in process of

rapid development. Much man-power is still necessary, and some of it may possibly be a permanent requirement in production, even in regard to purely physical-energy processes. But that requirement steadily decreases, and the proportion of man-power service which enters into the making of any given unit of produced output becomes less and less with every advance of power technique. And hardly a day passes without some such advance; constantly transferring to the power system processes previously dependent upon human energy.

Nor does it stop at the merely physical energy. In the supervision and regulation of the operations of the new powers there is a constant and rapid advance to automatism and self-regulation; while in many collateral activities on the business as well as the production side of the economy, such as those involving accountancy and reckoning, human service goes and the machine takes over; as the bank clerk, for instance, who only a year or two ago occupied what looked like one of the most assured sanctuaries for human service, has discovered.

The consequences of all this in the displacement of men were held back for some time in the earlier stages of the revolution by the fact that the power system was developed on a large scale in the one or two countries of its origin before it spread over the world generally. These countries had an almost unlimited range of outside markets into which to pour their products. They were for the moment in the position of being workshops for the world; and during that phase their activities were world activities concentrated in such comparatively small areas that, even though the bulk of their work was being done by the new powers instead of by human energy, their necessary employment of men expanded; the enormous increase in total output being more than sufficient to compensate for the diminished proportion of human service entering into each unit of output.

That, however, was only a transient phase. For reasons on which there is no need to enlarge here—they would be merely parenthetical to this study—this supply of goods to an outside world unequipped for supplying itself could not be simply a supply of consumers' goods.* The property-system conditions within which the whole business had to be conducted compelled it to develop largely into the supply of capital goods and the export of services for equipping the market countries for power-production on their own account. That equipment is now set up everywhere sufficiently to make it impossible for activities on the "workshop of the world" scale ever again to be concentrated in any few confined national areas. The power system has become a world system.

* See my *Economic Consequences of Power Production*, Chapter xiv, on this point.

Side by side with this geographical expansion by which such employment of men as the system requires is spread out more thinly over larger populations, the advance in the technique of power usage has been incessant; a process of constant further reduction in the amount of human employment required for any given output; a reduction so great as to enable the system to turn out heavily increased total outputs and still reduce employment.

There is no need to cumber the argument on this point with a mass of particulars. They will be found in overwhelming detail in any technical report or publication you care to consult. A single citation of figures, generalized from the data available over the whole industrial field, is quite sufficient to set out the concrete facts as to the rate of the human displacement in relation to output. The summary made from official sources for the decade 1920–30, and set out comprehensively (December 1932) in the *American Statistical Association Journal*, shows that for the same output for which, over the whole range of American industry, 100 men were required in 1920, only 68·2 men were required in 1929; and two years later, in 1931, only 65·2 men. In other words, the total output would have had to be increased by about half to carry the same number of men; anything less than such an increase involving a reduction in employment.

To these two developments—the world-wide

spread of power-equipment making it impossible for any part of the equipped area to command for itself the old "workshop of the world" scale of employment, and the constant advance of the technique itself making the hour of human service so increasingly productive that even if a return to "workshop of the world" demand for output were possible in any given area it could no longer prevent the displacement of men, and could only check the rate of that displacement in its own area by reducing the requirement for men elsewhere—to these two developments a third must be added.

Capital equipment of the more enduring sort—docks and harbours, roads and bridges, dams and buildings and all sorts of heavy constructional work—and even of the less but still in some degree durable sort in machinery and apparatus—has been carried to the point at which it does not require the same scale of activity in replacement and upkeep as was required for the original furnishing.

In the nature of things, that decline to a lower scale of activities in the production of capital goods and services must continue. For you cannot go on scrapping and rebuilding the heavy constructional bases of industry as a regular device for making employment possible. Even in an economy which gives to the mass of the people no right to live except by incessant labour, there are some things which must be regarded as durable. Salesmanship, under the pressure of keeping trade and employment going, may goad the world into creating work for itself by changing the fashion of its millinery twice a week. But the heavy industries are quite another story. The furnishing of the world with capable equipments has, in fact, already gone beyond the point at which they can be utilized within a property economy; a large proportion of them are standing idle or used only up to a fraction of their capacity.

The capacity of a property system to utilize the capital equipments it sets up depends, of course, upon its capacity, within its restrictive buying and selling procedure, to distribute profitably to itself the final output of consumers' goods from its capital equipment; and a full consideration of that buying and selling capacity belongs to a little later stage of our inquiry, when we have to consider the impact of abundance on a property economy. At the moment what we are concerned with is the displacement of men.

It is only comparatively recently—not, in fact, until well into this century—that these developments have carried the system to the stage at which the various set-offs against the displacement of human service which were operative in the earlier stages have quite definitely ceased to be able to set it off any longer. Increasing displacement has now become the permanent and regular condition of carrying on by the old procedures. Larger and larger masses of men are excluded from productive activities altogether, and still larger masses only part-time and precariously utilizable.

Already, under this dispensation, over a hundred millions of the world's disinherited, according to the estimate of the League of Nations, are scrapped in chronic unemployment; and no man who has any understanding at all of what the economic forces are which have scrapped them can be under any illusion as to their ever getting back. On the contrary, the probability is that if the system continues we shall look back in ten years' time to the fact that there were only a hundred millions of them as evidence of the enviable prosperity of these days. The steel-trade "boss," whom I heard discussing unemployment with a group of business men at Pittsburgh recently, put the plain truth about it. "Damn these fellows," he said. "They're scrap. There's millions of them we shall never have any possible use for in a power age; and we mustn't either shoot them or leave them to starve."

With which development the economy that gives to the mass of humankind no right to live except by rendering to the property system service which the property system no longer requires from them ceases to be merely a hardship and becomes a lunacy at large in the affairs of mankind.

## CHAPTER EIGHT

LET us now look for a little at the second of the major changes which the coming of power production has made in the physical realities of human economy; the change of productive activity from a mainly individual to an almost entirely communal process. Is the property system any more capable of adjustment to that change than it is to the transformation of production from a man-power to a non-human energy process?

In its origins, and for the immemorial generations of a world of peasant labour and handicraft, the property system was a quite simple direct appropriation from the community of services and products for direct usage by the lordships established over the community life. The right to make that seizure was, as we have noted, not dependent on any financial device. Nor is it now. It was, and still is, a basic property right; a right implicit in the property claim over the community's opportunities to produce; axiomatic in the institution of property.

But while it remains essentially the same thing, it is not quite the same *simple* thing.

In the old peasant and handicraft ages the supply of the all-round needs of community life was in local products drawn from local resources. What the property system got was the delivery to it of actual usable goods for the direct service of life; supplies from outside being a quite negligible margin in the infancy of commerce to which a world without effective transport was necessarily confined.

In such circumstances, each separate local lordship had what was for all practical purposes a complete and self-contained economy of living to handle; and within the range of a single feudal estate the planning and co-ordination of supplies to meet the general requirements of the estate life, according to the class standards of permitted usage which the property system stood for, was a simple business of apportioning the actual supplies.

All that way of living has now become physically impossible; a thing practically extinct in human economy. Except at the remote outlying frontiers of civilization, no local community in a world of power-production any longer produces its own all-round supplies for itself.

The productive energy required to place a simple single final product at the disposal of any individual consumer has, under power conditions, been split up into thousands of separate specialized operations spread about all over the world. Only a very small part of that energy is applied at the finishing point, the point of output of the completed usable product. The main work of producing any final utility is preliminary to that; a vast ramification of preparatory operations in the extraction, transport and processing of materials; the construction and equipment of power houses and power plants; with innumerable accessory materials, and equipments for the equipment, coming in all along the converging lines at every stage away back to raw materials virgin in natural resources; and in the background of all such provision for any particular final utility, a vast constructional provision of the basic things in transport and power for sustaining the system as a whole, without which as part of its available equipment every separate specialized activity in the whole process would be paralysed.

Even great nations, unless very exceptionally placed for raw materials, have ceased to be self-providing. All the world works before any one of us gets supplied with any of the ordinary things of individual daily use. Whole provinces are given over to specialization on little contributory bits of our daily needs; coal or steel or cotton or what not. And even when it comes to the converging of all these preparatory activities to the point at which a final usable product is completed, the specialization persists. No local community draws from the general system the prepared materials and equipment for producing its all-round supplies of final products, and then completes the process for itself. It specializes on some small single product; and we get huge industrial areas concentrating on the making of boots and shoes or the assembly of automobiles, and special communities of workers segregated for the supply of such minutiae as mustard or of needles and fish-hooks.

The productive energy of a local community has ceased utterly to be a complete economy of human living. It has become quite incapable, by reason of these power developments, not only of serving itself with its all-round requirements, but of carrying the production of any single thing, even as simple a thing as a match to light its pipe with, through all the operations and services which enter into its make-up as a final product.

The physical reality of production has thus become a communal process, in which no specialized activity has any separate self-contained utility. Utility is in the final product as the synthesis in which the whole process, from raw materials downwards, becomes a single organic unity of human effort in production, of which all the specialized activities are co-ordinated parts. But while this revolution has taken place in the physical reality of things, for property purposes each of these specialized sub-processes and interdependent activities through whose co-ordination the production of a final product is effected, is a separate property unit carried on to secure a separate property output for itself.

From each such separate business unit the property system still gets the output delivered to it in the old ownership way. But in a form quite unusable, either by the owner or by the working community under his immediate lordship. What each separate ownership gets is a mass delivery of some one special product, or of some special part or fragment of a product, or portion of an apparatus for producing or moving some fragment of a product to its further stage in the general co-ordination.

The world's work is thus carried on in separate units of property organization within which exclusive property rights are created over particular outputs; but the particular outputs themselves have no longer any exclusive utility value at all. So far as the physical facts are concerned, they have become elements of a single organic unity of production with a vital sequence of relationship to one another in the make-up of a final utility; and are quite as useless to their immediate groups of producers and owners as they are to the community generally, unless they are incorporated in that sequence.

In this entirely new set of physical realities two separate and wholly different problems arise. In any case, there arises from this change which power-production has made in the physical process by which final usable products are prepared and carried to completion, a new problem of planning and co-ordination which no human economy has ever before had to face; a problem which, under power-producing conditions, any economy, whether it be a property economy or an economy of production for use, must take in hand and deal with.

But it would present itself to two such different economies in a wholly different character. To a social economy producing for use and having its own natural sources of production at its own communal disposal, all this business of getting the related parts of a communally spread but organically single producing process effectively co-ordinated, would present itself as a problem of physical realities only; a problem of skilled management and administration in arranging the movement of actual materials and equipments so as to ensure that they get to their appropriate place at every stage in the production-for-use sequence. A problem as exclusively physical in character as putting the pieces of a jigsaw puzzle together into the unity of the single picture in which all the fragments the design has been cut up into are merged.

Our producing system, under power conditions, has become just such a communal merging of many specialized fragments of a single utility process into their unity of design in final products; and the only problem of planning and management which a consumer economy would have to face, would be that of fitting the pieces into this co-ordination, in which alone any of them mean anything; a problem wholly unrelated to property claims, and therefore wholly outside the entanglements of finance; a physical problem throughout.

A production-for-use economy, moreover, would not regard the utility design in production as being completed with the production of the material goods. The material goods would still mean nothing in final utility until human life itself, as the final product constantly sustained and renewed by the usage of the goods, comes into the picture and makes the utility productive design complete and intelligible. And just as in the intermediate activities by which goods-products become the raw material for this final production the whole problem of a consumer economy is the physical problem of having the materials and equipment in place when and where wanted, so also in the completing process of passing the goods on into usage. Given the use purpose in production, no other problem can arise at this stage any more than in the preparatory stages other than the physical problem of skilful management in moving the goods where they are needed; the whole economy being within the framework of life as a physical reality of producing and using; producing *for* using.

But a property economy has a very different purpose to serve when it sets out to adjust its procedure to the new physical reality of production as a communal process. It has to pursue its *property* purpose within this new framework of physical realities. And since physical realities are unescapable, it is under compulsion to fit the physical set-up of its producing procedure into the communal utility design of the new producing process. That is the imperative of the facts; for not one of the sub-processes and specialized functions through which the new production provides human life with utilities from natural resources could be carried on at all except in the sequence of the communal utility-producing process. Each such sub-process must get the set-up for its own functioning from, and pass its own specialized contribution into, the general communal process. They remain separate property units, creating exclusive property for their owners in their specialized outputs; but as producing units they have become completely disconnected from direct utility, which is now only achievable as the synthesis of communal effort.

The essential physical purpose of production is utility; in a property economy as in any other. The property claim on goods is a claim on usable goods for the maintenance of an owning class. And since, under power-producing conditions, the goods actually handed over to particular owners in the multifarious specializations of communal production are not directly usable for maintenance, the problem of the property system is to ensure their translation into maintenance. That is to say, into a claim *on final products*, the output into which all the maintenance-utility purpose in production has been synthesized.

The problem of planning and co-ordination which the property system has to face in adjusting itself to the new communal producing process is, therefore, a different problem altogether from that of securing the greatest possible physical effectiveness in producing the final utilities. It is the problem of so co-ordinating the separate property claims which have become disconnected from utility by the new process as to ensure that when the final utility is completed in production, it shall come into existence as property, with all the property claims accumulated against it during the preparatory processes effectively assertable over it against the consumer community. A problem of property titles and not of physical realities at all.

What has to be effected is that all the physically intricate movement of goods through all the stages of production shall be kept subject to such conditions as will safeguard the separate property claims asserted over each fragment of the goods during production right away down from raw materials to finished products, and make the final assignment of the completed goods to consumers conform to the property claims thus incorporated into them.

And that is a problem, not in the physical realities of our economy, but in the finance accountancy of the property system. Our modern complex money-system is the co-ordinating device for carrying the property title in this way through the labyrinth into which power-production has thus transformed the original simplicity of appropriating for direct use the output of small self-contained peasant and handicraft communities.

The sole function of a money system is to provide the accountancy for thus carrying property titles through to final utility products. It has become very intricate and involved, because the physical facts to which it has to relate its accountancy—the actual movements of goods and services through the process by which maintenance-utilities are finally completed—have become very intricate and involved. But its sole essential function is quite clear and simple: the accountancy evaluation of the property rights at every stage in these complex transactions, and the price-marking of every completed product with the aggregate of the property claims thus entered up against the consuming rights of the non-propertied working life of the community during its production.

* * * * *

A very brief parenthesis is needed at this point. The average man easily loses all sense of purpose or direction in studying the complex detail of a finance system; and it is vitally important to any real understanding that we get a clear grasp of the essential simplicity of the thing. The formula for any understanding about money is simply this: that money, and all the finance procedure by which money is created, issued, and permitted to be used, is never anything other than an accountancy of the actual property rights which are distinctive of the particular social structure in which the money is functioning. Its one purpose is to carry the accountancy of the property claims intact through whatever complexity of exchanges goods may have to pass in the process of distribution. Into whatever maze of operations a monetary system may extend, in all its relations to debt, as a "store of value," or an instrument for effecting savings and investment, every operation will be found on scrutiny to be merely accessory to this central governing purpose for which money exists.

## CHAPTER NINE

We have already seen something of the finance accountancy by which these property claims are entered up. It is, however, necessary to carry the scrutiny a little further.

If I may use Mr. Stuart Chase's illuminative descriptive phrasing of what has happened to the property system under power-producing conditions, it is this—that the value of the goods appropriated as property by the owner of any of the community's producing opportunities is no longer their direct "serviceability" to him, but their "vendibility."

He cannot use them for his own requirements. Their physical character is such that they can only be used by their widespread dispersal into the general human economy. But their intended usage within a property economy is *his* usage; and until the coming of power-production the property system delivered them over to him as physical utilities for his direct usage. But although they have become directly unserviceable to him, they are still delivered over to him as his possession, his exclusive property and means of living. He must, however, conform to the imperative of the physical facts; his property must be dispersed into widespread usage other than his own. But not by *giving* it away into that usage, and thereby surrendering his property title to use and enjoyment in it. Dispersal, yes; but only such dispersal as will preserve his property claim upon it as a means of living. It is by *selling* his special but unserviceable property that he gets it translated into equivalent supplies of the things he *can* use; serviceable possessions, in accordance with the essential purpose and the original practice of the property system in delivering the output of the community's producing activities over to him. And however intricate the processes of this "trading" may be, they will be found on scrutiny to be never anything other than means for achieving this essential and central purpose of the whole business; the translation of property from vendibility to serviceability.

What the property system requires for this conversion of each owner's directly unusable special possessions into an equivalent supply of general goods for all-round living is that there should be, firmly and legally established in general usage for passing goods into dispersal, a token form of property; not specifying ownership of particular goods, but a measure of the comparative dimension of property rights in any goods; into which token form any actual property in particular goods is convertible: with such conditions attached to the creation, issue and usage of the token as will ensure—no matter how remote or multiplied or intricate the dispersal movement of the actual goods may be—

that nobody shall be able to obtain goods during their dispersal except by presenting the equivalent property token for them, nor to obtain the token for that purpose except on the security of an actual property title, or by receiving it in disbursement from a property-owner who has so obtained it.

The dispersal of the goods into use must, at every point, be in the form of a market exchange of actual property for the property tokens; the essential purpose throughout being, not to put the consumer in possession of the goods he needs, but to recover for the property system, in token form, the serviceable-goods equivalent of the vendible goods it has to disperse in this way; the best market always being that which yields to the seller the most money for the fewest goods—the market in which the consumer fares worst.

Only when such a dependably established and safeguarded property token is obtainable for them can each separate ownership commit its special goods into the general world market-dispersal with the surety that, although it thus parts with its property—the goods themselves—the measure of its property rights over them will be preserved.

* * * * *

This is a distributive procedure in which, obviously, the real effective assignment of goods into permitted use and consumption is not in the market dispersal of the goods, but *in the prior assignment to consumers of the money which they can bring into the market.* The vital thing for the protection of the property rights during this market dispersal of the goods is, therefore, the procedure by which the consumer taking goods out of the market is permitted to obtain the tokens for taking them. For quite clearly the property system would come to immediate shipwreck if, when it has launched its property—the goods themselves—into the market, consumers were able to get possession of them there by having obtained the tokens for them except in strict conformity with the property rights established over them before they come into the market at all.

On this vital point the monetary procedure of the property system is fool-proof against being tampered with in the interests of the consumer. In the creation and issue of the tokens the monetary system has no dealings whatever with, nor even cognizance of, the consumer. What it creates and issues is exclusively a property token; and it creates and issues it *only to owners who can put up effective property securities for it.* Only by their disbursement of it in return for service rendered can the worker-consumer obtain it. By no other channel is it permitted to reach him.

Any unemployed man can have the facts as to this explained to him, possibly more plainly and probably more luridly than I am doing here, if he will call at the first bank he happens to be passing, and ask the manager to open an account to his credit as a consumer, so that he can be supplied with the necessary tokens for the goods he needs for current consumption. He may point out, quite unanswerably, that the goods he will thus obtain are completed goods passing through the process of distribution, that there is a great abundance of them, and that he has participated in the communal activities in production which brought them into being. But he will certainly not persuade the manager that his consumer needs are a sufficient reason for giving him the token authorizations to remove property from the market.

If the manager knows enough of the real procedures hidden behind the finance procedure to be able to give a reasoned reply to such an application, and has not swooned away at the effrontery of it, the reply would be that while it may be perfectly true that there is an abundance of goods and that the applicant has participated in their production, what he and the rest of the working community did in producing them was not to create for themselves any title whatever to use them. They were hired to create property rights; and all the goods so produced did in fact pass automatically, at their origins in production, not into social distribution, but into their owners' warehouses; from which they can only be permitted to be taken out into use on handing over to their owner the property token which will be valid to him for obtaining the other goods, the serviceable goods, into which his vendible goods are brought to market to be translated. And it could not be a valid guaranteed token for that purpose if the goods were to be removable from the market under any other than a property-rights title to them.

If the finance of a property system were to create *tokens* for goods for direct issue to anyone who does not possess property *rights* to goods in that equivalent, it would be destroying the purpose of its own existence. For in that case the token would cease to be a property token, and would become a consumer's claim to take goods out of the property system for nothing; precisely as if the owner had given the goods away in the first instance, or the consumer had acted as his own Bank of Issue and printed counterfeit tokens for himself stealthily in his own attic.

The operative cause-and-effect sequence in this matter is not that the penniless consumer is short of goods because he is short of money. He is short of money because he has no property right to goods, and is, therefore, not entitled within a property economy to the token for them; any more than a man who has not deposited a hat in the cloakroom is entitled to a cloakroom ticket authorizing him to remove a hat from it. It is true that he may have produced the actual physical goods; but production as a physical process has nothing whatever to do with property economics. It is *the property right* in the goods which is the hat in the finance cloakroom; and the physical production of goods gives to the working mass of mankind no such property right over them. The penniless (because propertyless) consumer can only obtain the token by having it disbursed to him in the course of producing further property rights for an employer to whom the money has been issued in the orthodox way.

This procedure, by which money can only make its original appearance as an issue of tokens to the property system on the security of its property rights over all output, and can only reach consumers through the disbursements which the property system makes of it in the course of further production, is a completely effective property safeguard. The general working community can make no inroad upon the property which ownership launches into the market under these conditions, beyond what is disbursed to them for maintenance by the property system itself in this way.

And having thus secured the market against any obligation to deliver goods to the general population beyond the maintenance assigned to its hirelings, the property system should, according to the finance reckoning, be able to proceed safely to what from its point of view is the real business of marketing—the conversion of the surplus from the unserviceable form in which power-production delivers the goods to each separate owner into a real use-and-enjoyment possession through the market exchanges which money as a property token enables the various owners to make with one another.

* * * * *

So far, therefore, as the registration of its claims is concerned, the property system has succeeded remarkably well in adjusting its procedure to the new communal character of production. Through these highly ingenious finance reckonings and money procedures, it carries its scattered unserviceable property rights into a synthesized charge against final products, in quite effective accord with the utility-synthesis in the final product which has been made in the physical facts. Every separate property claim is completely provided with an accountancy for its final market realization in utilities. And if the change which has been made in the physical realities were confined to this one matter of making production a communal process, but with only the old scarcity of output, the property system would no doubt be able to effect a market realization of its property purpose by finance reckoning as stable as it ever effected it by direct appropriation of utilities.

But the communal power-process in production

is not a scarcity process. It is its essential nature that it can only work to produce abundance. And it is to a consideration of the shattering effect of the new abundance upon this market realization of the property purpose that we must now turn for the completion of our inquiry.

# CHAPTER TEN

NOTE in the first place that in all this procedure we have been examining the real ultimate purpose of the property system is to get possession of serviceable goods for use and consumption.

In actual practice, the basic purpose of productive activities *in any economy* is necessarily a utility purpose, and the final value it sets itself to create is a serviceability value. Serviceability, the maintenance of human life and the satisfaction of human needs—human life would perish from the world if that ultimate rationality were lacking in its activities. . . . So that it remains true, even in a property economy, that the only real product is human life, and that production can be no other in its final purpose than production for use.

What the property system does is to put a class interpretation upon these fundamental realities of life; a class limit upon their application. It is a consumer and a utility economy only in relation to its own class claim on the world's resources; and, by the very fact that it is a class claim, and therefore exclusive, it is anti-consumer in relation to the general life, the non-propertied working life of the world.

Its pursuit of serviceable possessions is an active declaration of the truth that the only final product is human life; but all its procedure is an insistence that this means the human life of the propertied class only. It produces for use; but only for the use of the owning class against the general community. The rest of us, the mass of mankind, are, like its cattle, only servitors in the property organization of the world's life; having to be fed as its cattle have to be fed, because we would become disabled for servitude without it; but with no admitted footing of human right to live in its economy other than the right we share with its cattle of being so fed while an owner requires our service for his profit. And if that seems a harsh way of putting it, none the less it is the stark realism of human relationships within a property economy, as you can verify for yourself by trying to write down in clear definition what other footing than that of a cost which the property system has to incur (until it can get a cheaper non-human mechanism to displace us in rendering the service it needs) we do in fact possess within its economy.

* * * * *

The system is breaking down in general world confusion, because the copious abundance which power-production thrusts upon the world cannot be passed through these class channels of distribution.

The manifest governing purpose in the entire lay-out which the existing economy provides for human life and its activities is to keep in being a class structure of human society on a basis of property rights over the natural resources and producing opportunities of the general community; and so to secure the class control over the flow of produced supplies into use which lordship over the opportunities for producing them establishes. And while the output of an age of scanty producing powers could be assigned into use in that way, the output of our new producing powers cannot.

That our confusions are often made worse than they need be by stupidity in management and the creation of difficulties which might be avoided, is true enough. There are many such minor reformist opportunities within the property system. But these minor stupidities are merely incidental and unimportant. They may aggravate our trouble at any given moment; but they do not originate it, and the smoothing of them out would not remove it. It is in the clash of essential character and purpose between the property system and power-production that the trouble arises; the clash between forces which are innately irreconcilable. Producing powers on the one hand which can only work to ends of leisure and abundance in human life, and on the other hand a social structure whose definite design and function is to obstruct the passage of leisure and abundance into the general life and keep them confined to a class enclosure. It is in the very nature of our new producing powers that the leisure and the abundance they create cannot be so confined.

For they do not, it must be repeated with emphasis, *merely offer us the chance of leisure* and abundance. By the very law of their nature, if we use them at all, they *force* leisure and abundance upon us. They throw human labour out of requisition. And within the extent to which it is still called for they give a more and more abundant output to every hour of its required exercise.

Leisure and abundance are great and good gifts which a sane race of people would take sanely and use for the endowment of a general life of cultural activities; the great new advance in human civilization for which the new powers have cleared the way and given the means. If, however, we do not choose so to receive them, none the less we are compelled, from the moment the new powers in production become the physical realities of our economy, to receive them in some form.

The peoples of the world still choose to receive them within the property economy of the old class social structure. With the result that we get the leisure in the form of resourceless unemployment, and the abundance as a congestion of stocks for which the marketing procedure of the property system provides no adequate passage into use. The new powers cannot be used for the narrow purposes of a class society without thus turning into curses and disasters the great and good gifts of which they might be the carriers to the life of all mankind.

The property system cannot pass abundance through its markets. The only passage it can provide is a price-passage, constructed for the purpose of safeguarding the property rights over the goods and restricting their passage into the general life accordingly. And the appearance of copious plenty in its markets is a horror to it; for the price-passage cannot carry plenty; under the weight and volume of any sort of abundance prices are smashed and the market broken.

Hence the constant obsession of the property system to safeguard its markets from plenty; the burning and ploughing in and dumping into the sea of supplies, needed urgently enough by armies of consumers, the unloading of which on the market would knock down prices to a point at which the recovery of the property claim on the supplies becomes impossible.

To this same end of holding up prices so as to secure the property profit against the consuming needs of the world, production itself is restricted, and every device of economic localism is put into force for preventing the appearance of goods in the market from outside sources.

The property system is a scarcity economy; and the appearance of plenty in its markets is always a danger signal to it.

The capacity of power-production for unloading leisure and abundance upon mankind has developed incessantly and at an almost incredible rate of expansion during the past century; and our economic history during that period has been the record of the inability of the property system to stand up to the new conditions. Its economic lay-out of restricted little channels for the flow of goods—the channel of costs (which must be kept as small as possible), through which alone supplies can reach consumers, and the automatic overflow of any surplus into the property channel—is a lay-out constructed to catch such feeble drippings of cultural leisure as trickled down the rocks in an age of scarcity, and convey them into the pint pot receptacle of property rights reserved for a class. . . . And now suddenly here is Niagara pouring and thundering down into this little toy lay-out of conduits for scarcity; with shattering results upon its little market arrangements for doling out scarcity to mankind in general ("keeping costs down") and preserving the meagre surplus for itself in incessant fear that there will not be enough to go round if everybody is not compelled to economize in use and consumption.

The highly ingenious finance reckonings by which ownership, having in the first instance had its market safeguarded against any effective demand being made upon it for the delivery of goods to the general mass of people beyond their allotted maintenance, has been provided with an accountancy for passing the surplus into use-dispersal within its own class enclosure, have broken down utterly. It is an abundance beyond any such limited class power of consumption. If production is allowed to go on beyond a meagre fraction of producing capacity, the property market goes to pieces under the pressure. The abundance becomes an inundation, a glut and congestion of unsaleable goods for which ownership cannot make a market itself; and cannot throw into general consumption without smashing the essential class-distribution character of its lay-out of costs and prices. If production were allowed for only a few weeks to operate up to the full capacity of the existing plants and equipments, every market in the world would be ruined. The basic property requirement, the delivery of the price to the seller, which the market exists to serve, is rendered impossible whenever the market is flooded with plenty.

* * * * *

The economic history of the past century has been the history of this swamping of the property price-market by abundance in depression after depression, each following more swiftly on the heels of the last, and each more world-wide in the devastating economic confusion into which it has thrown the affairs of mankind. It is a market which cannot give passage into the lifestream of the world for the plenty which the new producing energies of the world force upon it. The decisive fact in every depression is the smashing of the price-channel through which it passes goods to consumers, whenever the flow of supplies goes beyond the scarcity volume the channel is designed to carry. In relation to the real capacity of power-production to serve human life, the operations of the property market are like an attempt to run the Mississippi through a four-inch pipe.

In the depression production slows down; producing plants stand idle; many of them are scrapped; the small investors who had been hoping by savings to establish themselves inside the property enclosure are jolted out of it in as large numbers as possible by capital depreciation; and accumulated stocks are in some measure depleted. When the process has been carried far enough to re-establish comparative conditions of scarcity, a temporary apparition of recovery shows itself—until production gets going again.

That has been the process so far; the "trade cycle" which the economist apologists for the property system have been at such great pains to persuade the world to regard as the natural and, therefore, unavoidable rhythm of human affairs; with nothing else to be done about it but to carry on as cheerfully as possible through each depression phase until we reach the next recovery phase, which is always just round the corner. A rhythm, apparently, which is to go on for ever, with periodic confusion as a natural recurring experience for human life in a world of abundant resources for human well-being and security.

All of which, of course, is sheer illusion. There has been no rhythm for eternal recurrence in these depression and recovery phases through which the property economy has been passing since the coming of power-production. What has been manifest in it is a steadily increasing dominance of the forces making for depression in these "cycle" movements. The failure of the market to function has become more marked at every recurring phase, in direct relation to the growing capacity of the new producing powers to unload plenty upon it.

It has been the rhythm of collapse; the rhythm of the spinning top losing its momentum; a rhythm which begins with a slight movement out of balance and a good recovery, and then another and another swerve progressively more and more out of balance with recoveries less and less effective, until the final swerve carries it to collapse beyond recovery.

We have reached the stage in this movement at which depression has ceased to be periodic and has become continuous. There will be no recovery; the system is in collapse. Its collapse does not, of course, mean that human life may not have to stagger along after a fashion under the continued operation of its forms and procedures for an indefinite period. Its forms and procedures will continue so long as we choose to continue them and to endure the consequences. But its collapse is none the less a fact, in that its continuance can now be only a continuance of uninterrupted depression, in which markets incapable of functioning, unemployment, and all the aggravated human discomfort and insecurity hitherto periodic in its working, have become its constant and worsening accompaniment.

With the rate at which our now available but still constantly growing powers of production, once they get going at all, pour out products beyond the carrying capacity of the property price-market, any beginning of recovery which set them going, even to the smallest extent that could be called a recovery—and recovery means nothing else than setting them going—would be swamped almost immediately into more overwhelming confusion than ever.

* * * * *

What all this means for us in constructive action is production planned and carried on as the co-operative enterprise of the community itself for the direct provision and issue into use of all things needful to its life; a new economy of human living for which the essential foundation is direct and unqualified community command over the natural resources from which all things needful to life have to be drawn.

Nothing short of this purpose of basic reconstruction in the economic life of the world will serve us for effective escape from the consumer disabilities which the property economy imposes upon us. It is a matter, not of purchasing power, nor of issuing credit to consumers, not any other accountancy futility for dodging the essential and undodgible anti-consumer consequences of producing goods as property rights to begin with instead of as community supplies; but of the social handling of the real things themselves.

Social ownership of the natural resources, and planned co-operative social activity in producing supplies from them; producing for direct use up to the full measure of producing capacity and of the needs of the community; only upon such a co-operative commonwealth foundation can the economy of human living get back to reason and reality. The reality of human economy as a process of producing and using, and the common sense of regarding the use and consumption of supplies as the only sane rational purpose of producing them at all.

# APPENDIX

## "A+B"

I HAVE kept the actual text of this brief study closely to its single purpose. It is an attempt to make our present confusions intelligible by a realist approach to the facts, and in that way to reach a clear central understanding of the essential relationship of our existing property economy to the consumer needs of mankind. And I have been at some pains not to obscure that direct issue by making any diversion into the by-ways.

It may, however, be interesting and helpful—not by way of adding to the case here presented, which is, I think, complete in its essentials, but by way of illustration—if we take one of the outstanding monetary reformist illusions now in current discussion, and as a footnote to our inquiry, examine it closely in the light of the conclusions to which our main study has led us. It is an examination which, I think, shows pretty conclusively how the sense of direction which such a central understanding gives us can save us from wandering off the main track of realities into the jungle of tempting illusions with which our way out of our present confusions is beset.

* * * * *

I take for this purpose the A+B theorem put forward by Mr. C. H. Douglas. It has attracted a good deal of attention; and since most of its critics share with Mr. Douglas the basic property concepts on which his proposal is founded, the reply to him has, naturally, not been very convincing. A considerable number of people, possibly at the moment a growing number, have come to accept his Social Credit gospel as a Messianic solution of our consumer problem, capable of being put into operation, as he himself constantly insists, without disturbing the established property system.

The theory upon which he bases his case is that the rate of flow of prices from the producing system is always greater than the rate of flow of purchasing power to consumers; so that when the final commodities come into the market the total money possessed by individuals—the aggregate of purchasing power which has been distributed throughout the community—is always insufficient to meet the total prices for which the goods must be sold if the costs entered up against them in the finance accountancy of their production are to be recovered in the price.

It is by this *aggregate* shortage of money, he argues, that we are disabled from getting goods into use and consumption. It is not simply that certain individuals or even classes are short of money; the theorem, it should be noted, does not deal with disparities as between individual consumers in the distribution of purchasing power. It is the aggregate of money possessed at any given moment by *all* individuals of all classes which, according to Mr. Douglas, is always below the total costs which have been charged against all the goods in the market at that moment, and therefore below the cost-price which is the minimum that must be recovered from the consumer if the producing system is to avoid bankruptcy.

And this shortage, he claims, is brought about by faults of procedure, not in the control of production but in the control of finance; and can be corrected within the monetary system without affecting the control of production or the property system at all.

Now, let the reasoning which Mr. Douglas offers in proof of this theory speak for itself. It would be unfair, when one believes it to be sheer illusion and no proof at all, to attempt to paraphrase it. The following, therefore, is his case in full as he himself sets it out:—

> "To see whether this" (i.e. the shortage of aggregate purchasing power) "is so, it is necessary to examine the method by which money comes into the hands of consumers on the one hand, and prices are attached to goods on the other.
>
> "Suppose that 'A' has £1,000 (Stage 1), and

that he pays that £1,000 away to ten men for the purpose of building a factory. To eliminate unnecessary complications, let it be assumed that the land and materials are free.

"When the ten men have built 'A's' factory, they have 'A's' £1,000 and 'A' has a factory which cost £1,000 (Stage II).

"Regarding these ten men in their consuming aspect, £1,000 has passed over to the consuming or positive side of the ledger, and a factory which *cost* £1,000 has appeared on the negative side of the ledger as a component of a subsequent *price*. So far so good. There is a balanced equation.

"Now, let it be imagined that these ten men, who collectively have £1,000, buy the factory from 'A' at cost. 'A' now has his £1,000 back again where it started from, and the ten men have a factory priced at £1,000. Note particularly that only as an organization have they obtained delivery of the factory. They have not taken bits of it home (Stage III).

"Suppose now that 'A' employs the same ten men to build £1,000 worth of machinery. They have the same £1,000 back again, and 'A' has machinery which *cost* £1,000 (Stage IV).

"Let it be supposed that 'A' again allows the ten men to buy the machinery from him at cost. 'A' has the original £1,000 back again, and they have got a factory and machinery which cost

£2,000 (Stage v). No one has any money except 'A.'

"Now suppose that 'A' agrees with these ten men to form a company to build motor cars in the factory and with the tools covered by the previous stages; and pays out his £1,000 to new men in wages. 'A' and the original ten men are now capitalist employers. At the end of Stage VI there will be motor cars of which the wages cost was £1,000, and the new workmen will have 'A's' £1,000. If it be imagined, to make the hypothesis as simple as possible, that the factory and tools were worn out in the process of producing the motor cars, and as in all the previous stages any question of profit be neglected, the owners of the factory and tools will say that the motor cars cost £3,000.

"But nobody in the story possessed £3,000; and there are only two ways in which the motor cars which have been produced can be distributed: either they must be exchanged for the £1,000 which is in the hands of the workmen, and which 'A' wants back, or £2,000 must be obtained from some completely new source.

"It will be noticed that the difficulty arises at the point where the goods produced leave the industrial organization to be delivered to individuals—the ultimate consumer—and the difficulty takes the form that the individual cannot pay the price which the industrial organization would appear to be obliged to charge.

"It is quite clear that in the illustration there is no difficulty in seeing where the 'equity' of the final ownership of the motor cars resides; two-thirds of it is in the company, and one-third with the workmen. But that does not help matters. The transfer of the motor cars to the actual user can only take place by a reverse transfer of money. And the only people who have money are the second ten working workmen, and *they only have one-third of the amount necessary.*"

At this point Mr. Douglas writes Q.E.D. to his demonstration. "The result," he says, "to be derived from this investigation therefore is that even if all prices were equivalent to production costs only, the money extant in the hands of individuals would collectively be far less than the collective prices of available goods." And since to such "production costs only" profits must be added to make a true estimate of what actual prices are, the situation in respect of shortage of aggregate purchasing power is, he points out, "thereby still further worsened."

In his particular illustration he works it out, as you see, to a final outcome in which the flow of prices that have to be charged for the goods is three times as great as the whole of the money available for buying them; and since the same thing happens in every industrial unit, the position can be expressed in a general formula. This formula is the "A+B theorem," and runs thus:

> All industrial payments may be divided into two groups:
>
> Group A.—All payments made to individuals (wages, salaries and dividends).
>
> Group B.—All payments made to other organizations (raw materials, bank-loans and other non-personal costs).
>
> Now the rate of flow of purchasing-power to individuals is represented by A; but since all payments go into prices, the rate of flow of prices cannot be less than A+B. Since A will not purchase A+B, a proportion of the product at least equivalent to B must be distributed by a form of purchasing-power which is not comprised in the descriptions grouped under A.

"These considerations," he points out, "make it clear that the continuance at all of the industrial and finance system depends upon the influx of new money"; and on that he proceeds to the second part of his case, in which he makes proposals for dealing with such a situation. This new money which he thinks is required to make up the shortage of purchasing power now comes, he says, from the banks; and what he proposes is that their method of creating and issuing it as a banker's debt-charge against the producing system should be superseded, and a new method adopting for creating it as Social Credit and issuing it to the consumer public, partly by limiting prices below accounted costs (the actual new money in that case being issued to the owners of industry to make up for the unaccounted costs), and partly by issuing it direct to the general consumer public as a social dividend.

* * * * *

With the detail of these proposals we need not concern ourselves for the moment. For they are proposals designed expressly to meet a defined situation; and if in fact that situation does not arise at all—if the situation which has actually to be met in our present economic confusions is found on scrutiny *not* to be the situation which A+B defines, but the very reverse of it—the proposals themselves necessarily cease to have any meaning or relevance. Our first business, obviously, is to test the validity of the basic theorem on which the proposals are founded. The question we have to examine is, therefore,—Is is true that the A payments made in the course of production to individuals as purchasing power, being a component of the final prices which must be collected when the final product is marketed, and remaining extant in the hands of individuals as purchasing power towards equating those prices, are insufficient to equate them because other payments made during production, the B payments not made to individuals but to organizations, have also been computed into the prices; and that the flow of cost-prices is in that way continuously greater than the flow of purchasing power for meeting them? Let us, therefore, turn our scrutiny upon the basic A+B demonstration of this foundation of the whole social credit case.

*  *  *  *  *

We have presented to us, as Stage I in the producing process, A with £1,000 and ten men with nothing, and A paying his £1,000 away to the ten men for building a factory. Stage II is the completion of the building; and, says Mr. Douglas, "when the ten men have built A's factory, they have A's £1,000 and A has a factory which cost £1,000."

Really? That A has the factory costing £1,000 is true enough. But that the men engaged to build it have A's £1,000 is not true at all. It is simple unadulterated nonsense. What has happened in fact is something completely different from a mere movement of money from A to the men. For what, one may ask, have the men been living upon while they have been building the factory?

The theory which Mr. Douglas seeks to establish—that the purchasing power distributed in the course of production should be "extant in the hands of individuals," extant in its character as consumer's purchasing power, when the final products (the ultimate motor cars in his illustrative case) resulting from the current work in respect of which it is paid out to individuals come into the market—no doubt requires that they should live upon nothing in the meantime; and this Mr. Douglas assumes them to have done when he presents them to us with the £1,000 still in their possession on the completion of the factory. But things do not happen like that in the real world. In actual fact, the £1,000 is disbursed to them for *current sustenance*, and is used during the currency of their work as purchasing power over *previously produced and currently available consumer-goods*. As effective purchasing power it does not operate, and is never intended to operate, as consumer-power for meeting the prices at which the ultimate motor cars will come into the market.

We must follow that up rather closely if we are to see with any clearness what it is that really happens in this factory-building preliminary stage of producing motor cars; what the flow of purchasing power from the producing system really is, and to what user-goods—the existing and available real things or the "credit" phantom of things as yet unmade—the flow of purchasing power is directed;

what A's £1,000, the money aspect of the transaction, does in fact stand for in the actual movement of real things; and what has happened to the money when the preliminary factory-building has been completed.

Let us be quite clear, to begin with, as to what the Social Credit proposals based on A+B aim at doing. Mr. Douglas's whole complaint is that when final products come into the market, the money paid out by the producing system during their production and entered up as costs against them, costs which are the components of their prices, is not extant as purchasing power in the hands of individuals, and that the goods therefore cannot be bought. And he blames the finance procedure for this disappearance of purchasing power. He accepts the basic property-system idea that the disbursement of purchasing power during production is a "credit" for goods that will appear later on; but he wants it to be issued as social "Credit" direct to consumers instead of by the present finance arrangements.

The crux of the whole matter is that in the world of realities the distribution of goods to consumers is always a matter of the current sustenance of life. And life can only be sustained by the use and consumption of real things; never by an accountancy of credit for the use and consumption of things which will not come into existence until some indeterminate future date. Unless the real things are already there and completed in production there is no current sustenance. Getting goods to consumers by distributing purchasing power to them which has to remain "extant in the hands of individuals" when the ultimate product of their current activities comes to market a year hence, is only possible in the dreams and illusions of monetary accountancy. In the physical realities of human life it is a grotesque impossibility. The purchasing power may be *accounted* as a credit for the future goods, but it can only be *used* as a permit to take existing goods. . . . And that is why, at the very outset of his A+B exposition, Mr. Douglas, being compelled by the exigency of his dream accountancy to treat A's payment of his £1,000 to the ten men as a credit equipment of the market with purchasing power against the prices which the market will have to carry when the future goods are unloaded into it, gets out of the world of realities altogether by ignoring current sustenance and assuming that they are still in possession of the £1,000 at the completion of their work of factory building.

It is obvious, therefore, that if we are to understand what really happens in this transaction, we must set up a framework of realities to begin with instead of the framework of mere accountancy which A+B starts with. Mr. Douglas sets the stage for the opening of the producing process by eliminating every reality. He rings up the curtain on a Stage 1 setting in which nobody appears but A with his £1,000 and a group of working people with nothing; the action of the play, in the A+B presentment of it, being that a factory comes into existence by the transfer of the £1,000 from A to the men. He ignores altogether the current sustenance of everybody concerned; although that, as we shall see, is the essential reality of the whole thing; the purpose running through the whole procedure of the general economy of which the factory-building is a component part being to secure the continuous distribution of this current sustenance *on a class-disparity basis.* It is true that he makes a concession to reality by admitting the necessary existence of land and materials, the omission of which would be too obviously grotesque. But he evidently has an instinctive sense of the danger of that admission to his case; for with that shrinking from realities which characterizes all monetary reform advocacy, he asks us to assume that land and materials are free, and can be "eliminated" as only introducing "unnecessary complication" into the working out of the essential action of the producing system in relation to the distribution and use of purchasing power. He also assures us that any question of profit throughout the whole transaction may be neglected for the same reason. And having thus eliminated every reality—for at no moment and in no possible way in all the reality of things in human economy does anything whatever occur other than the current usage by current human activities of already existing and currently usable things—he proceeds to develop his case unhampered by any embarrassing suggestion that the affairs of human life are anything other than figures in an accountancy of costs and prices related to the distribution into use of things not yet in existence at all.

What, then, is the actual realist Stage I lay-out for the beginning of the producing process? A factory has to be built. The components of the factory are the land, the materials, and the stores of current consumer goods for sustaining and equipping everybody concerned during the operation of building. Unless these things are there and available for use, either in natural resources or in completed products, the process of building the factory cannot begin. They must be there to start with. And they *are* there; but locked up in the property system, into which they were appropriated at their origins in production; and with prices tagged to them as the measure of the property claim upon them. A's £1,000 does not bring them into existence. It is simply the registered accountancy of his property claim over them up to that price measurement. It is the measure of his individual holding in the property system, and gives him the right to pick and choose from the general property system, to the extent of that measure, the particular goods required for building the factory; and so to change his property holding from its token form of money into a holding of specified actual goods. He takes his goods, therefore, and gives up his property-token, the money; which does not go outside the property system, but is simply transferred within it. In short, he makes what Mr. Douglas calls a B payment. The money which he disburses to his ten men is simply a permission to them, for purposes of convenience, to obtain direct delivery of that part of his holding in the property system which he requires in the form of consumer goods to sustain them while they are doing his work. And this also is in reality a B payment; and is in fact, as we shall see later, consolidated into a B payment before, as a cost, it enters into the price of the ultimate product.

It is *solely* for this release of already existing things from the general property system into their specific use—*solely* for meeting the claim of the property system over all goods before their use is permitted—that the money functions. With the actual work of production—the transforming of the various components into a factory by human effort applied to them on their being thus released into use—the money has no more to do than it has with the digestive processes by which the consumer goods, released into use in the same way, are transformed into human life and activity. The money is a function of the property rights only, the property rights over all the *opportunities* to produce—all the material components requisite for production, including current sustenance for everybody concerned—and not of any reality of producing and using at all.

*     *     *     *     *

The actual setting of the stage for beginning this factory-building operation is, therefore, as follows; taking X to represent the general property system:

> X in possession of the natural resources, materials, equipments and supplies of produced consumer goods, which in their aggregate constitute the community's total available current sustenance and enablement for producing the factory:
>
> A in possession of a property title to select from this general store of the community's resources, up to £1,000 measure—the money accountancy of his individual holding in the property system—the particular goods which the workers must have at their disposal for building the factory:
>
> the ten men possessing nothing.

At the end of this stage, when the factory is completed, the position is:

The ten men, as at the beginning, have nothing:

A has the factory and has parted with his £1,000 (i.e. his individual holding in the property system has been changed from an accountancy measure of general title—a property-*token* holding—into a specific holding of real things):

The property system has parted with certain consumer-goods and recovered A's £1,000 token measure of property rights back from the consumers, to whom it was only issued quite transiently for this prompt return into the property system; and has obtained the transformation of certain of its unworked materials into the higher-utility form of a constructed factory.

One other quite vitally important thing has also happened; but as its significance does not become fully manifest until the producing process of which the factory is only the initial stage comes to completion in final products, it can wait until our examination reaches that stage. At this point it need only be noted in passing. At the end of Stage 1 the property system has both the new factory and the money; but the individual property holdings have been transferred: A, who began with the money and no factory, now has the factory and no money; while the previous holders of the materials and the sustenance goods used during the workers' production of the factory have parted with their goods-holding and obtained a property-holding in the token form instead. What has happened, therefore, is that the property system has obtained a new factory in return for the current sustenance of the workers engaged, and has regained possession of the money, which was only circuited for a brief moment to the workers as a permit to obtain the consumer goods, and had to be returned at once to the property system for that purpose: the money transferred to the owners of the materials never passing outside the property system at all. But quite obviously one other thing *must* have happened; a quite imperative thing in the physical realities of life. For, just as at the outset, when A+B represents the workers as being in possession of the money when the factory is completed, the question which had to be asked was "What, then, have they been living on during the currency of the work?" so also, when it is represented that all the property system gets out of it is a new factory with no self-contained utility, and serving no consumer purpose in itself, the question which has to be asked is "What, then, have the owners been living on during this period?" For quite manifestly their current sustenance has also been going on; and has been as completely unrelated to "credit" for the final utility which will ultimately come of the new production as was the current sustenance of the workers; as, indeed, current sustenance for anybody must be in the physical reality of things. Nobody, owner or worker, has been living on an accounted credit for non-existent forthcoming goods: it has been current sustenance, the actual use and consumption of real things available for use and consumption. . . . In actual fact, ownership has not only obtained a new factory in return for the current sustenance of the workers. It has been getting its own current sustenance also out of the transaction; and in the general economy of which the factory-building is only a fragment, the factory-building operation has, as we shall see, been handing over to the property system, at the sole cost of the workers' sustenance, not only the new factory, but also its due quota of this general ownership sustenance.

It is in the next stage (Stage III in Mr. Douglas's presentment of his case) that the basic absurdity of the A+B reckoning begins to be clearly manifest. The opening assumption which Mr. Douglas makes at this stage is, of course, now seen to be quite untenable. He pictures the position thus—that the men, "who collectively have £1,000" when the factory is completed, buy the factory from A in order to provide him with the £1,000 necessary to employ them again to make £1,000 worth of machinery to put into it. Which, of course, is bosh. The men, in fact, have not got the money. The money is back again into the property system; and if A wants to finance the making of machinery—i.e., to draw £1,000 worth of existing property out of the property system in the form of sustenance goods for maintaining the men while they are making the machinery—he must either possess a further £1,000 token-holding in the property system, or he must pledge his factory or such other actual property as he may possess up to the £1,000 measure, as security for obtaining the money-tokens from the banking system, which is the general clearing-house for the property system in these matters.

Let Mr. Douglas, however, complete his statement of what happens in this machinery-making stage of the producing process before commenting upon it. Having equipped A with the £1,000 to finance the machinery-making in the manner described, the A+B argument asks us to note that "A now has his £1,000 back again where it started," and that when he disburses it to the men "they have the same £1,000 back again"; by which reckoning we are brought at the end of this stage to a position in which a factory equipped with machinery is carrying a cost of £2,000 as a component of a future price, and the only money anybody has to meet that price with is "the original £1,000"; and there is therefore a shortage of £1,000 in requisite purchasing power if the price is to be paid.

Now, if Mr. Douglas had not at the outset so

carefully eliminated from his reckoning all the realities, all the actual happenings in regard to current sustenance, he would surely begin to suspect something wrong with his case at this point. At the end of the first factory-building stage he found the position satisfactory. There was only this £1,000 involved, and only £1,000 entered as costs against the factory. "So far so good," said Mr. Douglas cheerfully at that point, "there is a balanced equation." But so far as the balance for which he is seeking is concerned—a balance of consumers' purchasing power extant in the hands of individuals against the price of the completed factory—it was not a balanced equation at all, even at that stage. What he seeks to do, throughout the whole Social Credit case, is to get money distributed in such a way as to ensure that the costs accounted against the goods during the course of production are balanced by an amount of money in the hands of individuals available for meeting the price-equivalent of the accounted costs when the goods come to market. And there was no such balance even at the first stage; and A+B was only able to demonstrate a balance by assuming that the money which had in fact been spent on current sustenance during the currency of the new work was still in the hands of the men when the work was finished. A palpable absurdity; the men were not in possession of any "extant" consumer power at all.

But if that was so even at the first producing stage, what have we now at the end of the machinery-producing stage? Still clinging desperately to his basic "credit" concept that money disbursed as purchasing power during a period of production is consumer credit for the product which will appear at the end of that period, Mr. Douglas again assumes that when the machinery is completed the men must be in possession of the money disbursed to them during the production period. But even that absurd assumption is insufficient to make a balanced equation at the end of this second stage. There is now an accounted cost of £2,000 against the factory and machinery; and still only the same old original £1,000 to set against it, and that £1,000 only in the A+B dream accountancy, and not in fact at all. For in actual fact the men, as in the first stage, have handed it back to the property system in return for a second period of current sustenance.

The same story, but with a further £1,000 shortage in the balance, is repeated in the A+B description of the final stage in the producing process—the making of the motor cars as the final utility product. "The original £1,000" is brought in again to finance this final process, and by the same method as before; the men, who are assumed to have it on the completion of the machinery, buying the machines from A with it. But this time

Mr. Douglas makes a change in the method of disbursing it to the final workers. He assumes that the original ten workers, having lived on nothing, and therefore been able to buy the factory and the machinery from A, are now, as a result of two short spells of employment, capitalists in possession of the factory and tools they were employed to make. They therefore form a company with A, who now has the £1,000, and a fresh ten workmen are employed to make the motor cars; and to them the same original £1,000 is again disbursed. They are again assumed to be in possession of it when the final products are ready for market.

But, he asks, how are they to be marketed? Who is to buy them? For there is now £3,000 accounted against them as costs to be recovered in prices. "But nobody in the story possessed £3,000," says Mr. Douglas. "The only people who have money are the final workmen, and they *have only one-third of the amount necessary.*"

The reality is, of course, that even this "one-third of the amount necessary" is not there. The final workmen, like the workmen in the two preceding stages, have used it for current sustenance while they were making the motor cars; and the conclusion of the whole matter is that when *any* final product makes its completed appearance nobody, so far as the A payments which were disbursed to consumers during its production are concerned, possesses the purchasing-power equivalent of the A payment component in the price.

* * * * *

Now, let us try to see clearly the facts as to this.

If Mr. Douglas's reasoning is correct, what he has proved (leaving out his pathetically futile effort to save a one-third remnant from the wreck of his theorem) is the exact reverse of the A+B conclusion. For what has happened in his illustrative case is, as you see, *the disappearance of the A flow of purchasing power* as a factor for equating the final price.

The A+B theory, let us remind ourselves, is that all payments made in the course of production may be divided into two groups: Group A, payments made to individuals (wages, salaries and dividends), and Group B, all payments to other organizations (materials, bank-loans and other non-personal costs): that the rate of flow of purchasing power to individuals is represented by A; but that since all payments, both in the A and B group, have to go into prices, A must be insufficient to purchase A+B. The A+B case is, therefore, that the shortage of purchasing power in the hands of individuals when the final product comes to market is due to the fact that *the B payments* are not in the effective possession of any purchasers.

But in his illustrative case, Mr. Douglas has included *only A payments*. He has asked us to assume that all materials have been free, and that the only payments made by the producing system are the direct A payments made to the workers. The flow of purchasing power has therefore been precisely equivalent to the flow of cost-prices. . . . And yet, when the final product makes its appearance at the end of the process, Mr. Douglas himself is compelled to admit a shortage of two-thirds of the purchasing power necessary to meet the cost-price. And in actual fact there is none of it at all left extant in the hands of individuals; the final ten workmen, whom he represents as possessing one-third of it, having in fact used it for current sustenance as in the preceding stages. By the time the final product is completed, the whole of the A payments—not just the two-thirds admitted by Mr. Douglas, but the A payments *in their entirety*—have vanished as extant purchasing power against the price which has to be recovered.

The A+B attempt to explain this shortage by running the same £1,000 through all the stages of production and asking us to believe that the workers have only had a recurring possession of the same thing each time, "nobody in the story" having ever had £3,000—as if the money were a corporeal real thing, like the slipper in the old round game of hunting it, instead of an accountancy for measuring out supplies of real things—is the sheer illusion of mistaking figures for things, by which all projectors of monetary schemes for correcting our economic evils are hag-ridden.

The flow of purchasing power during the producing process has been *the full equivalent* of the £3,000 accounted cost of the final products. The workers at each stage have not, as Mr. Douglas in effect represents them as doing, got their current nourishment by regurgitating their previously eaten food and eating it over again. It has been purchasing power over a £3,000 measure of consumer goods; and on being exercised as purchasing power has gone back into the property system as *£3,000 actual money*. Mr. Douglas's idea that nobody has possessed £3,000 in the whole story is all bunkum; as the owners of the consumer goods sold to the workers, if he could get them together into a general assembly and tell them that they had been fools enough to part with £3,000 of their property for £1,000, would very promptly assure him. And it has vanished out of the hands of individuals as purchasing power against the prices which have to be collected from the market when the final product makes its appearance, not because it has been cancelled, or the banking system has played obscure tricks with it, but because it has been *used*; and used in the only way in which the physical realities of life permit purchasing power issued to consumers to be used, not as credit for goods that are passing through production, but for obtaining currently available completed consumer-goods during the currency of the further production.

And what is true in Mr. Douglas's illustrative case is true of all production. The A payments issued directly to consumers while the production is going on, and entered into the costs of the forthcoming products—the payments which A+B represents as purchasing power that survives as an effective part-equivalent to the prices of future products—are in fact the payments which invariably disappear completely, and in the physical reality of things must disappear, *during* the production of the future goods; purchasing power which cannot survive to meet the prices of the future goods. Such payments, over the total of all industry, are the equipment of the working human life of the community for its current consumer needs, and are used accordingly. A fact so obvious that Mr. Douglas's repeated assertion that the group of workmen engaged on any prolonged productive operation like building a factory are in possession, when the operation is completed, of all the purchasing power which has been distributed to them during the period of their employment, has a grotesqueness about it the full flavour of which can probably only be relished by the man who falls out of employment when that job is finished or by the Public Assistance Committee which has to deal with his case.

All A payments thus disappear as consuming power over future goods; *as in the physical reality of things they must disappear.* For there is no such thing possible in physical reality as consuming power over future goods; use and consumption being physical acts only possible of performance in relation to existing goods. It is this utterly illusory "credit" idea of the distribution of purchasing power which is the essential absurdity of A+B. All its computations, all its talk of A payments and B payments, are an attempt to follow up the "credit" accountancy into next year in the vain expectation of discovering there some actual reality of relationship between present consuming power and future goods; a thing crazily absurd and fantastic in the world of fact.

When you say that A payments are made (purchasing power disbursed to individuals) what that means in actual happening is that real goods are placed at the disposal of consumers for their current sustenance; that people are, in fact, eating real dinners instead of feasting on the consumability of next year's as yet ungathered harvest. All the time, behind all this accountancy, nothing whatever happens in fact other than the real current use and consumption of goods already there; whether it be their final use for human sustenance or the active creative use of them as components in new products in preparation for future human sustenance. Nothing ever happens or can happen in the physical realities of human economy other than this continuous use and consumption of things already prepared for use and consumption.

The whole accountancy of costs and prices is a "credit" accountancy, and therefore a false accountancy; false because it makes the reckoning run in the reverse direction to the reality of things; the "costs" being the reckoning by which the current distribution of consuming power is carried forward into a price relation to future goods, whereas in its exercise consuming power can never have any sort of relationship whatever to future goods.

A+B, accepting the false reckoning, sets out to devise a new manipulation of the credit idea which will bring the physical realities of life into line with the "credit" accountancy, and make next year's harvest consumable here and now by calling the credit "social credit," instead of banker's finance. But a physical impossibility remains a physical impossibility, by whatever new name you call it, or in whatever new way you may render an accountancy of it. The essential A+B absurdity is that it is a "credit" accountancy, and therefore the accountancy of a physically impossible thing. And the essential fallacy of its reasoning is that, beginning as it does with an acceptance of the "credit" concept of purchasing power issued to consumers, it assumes that because the A payments by which it is issued must be carried forward as "costs" to survive in the *quantity measurement*, the figure, of prices reckoned against future goods, they must, therefore, also be found surviving in *their actual character of consuming power* against those prices; and that if they are found to be insufficient to meet the total price when that price comes to be collected from consumers, that is because other factors represented by B payments, which are not purchasing power to individuals, have been added to the price; the conclusion being that a new supply of purchasing power, still as "credit" against future prices, must be issued to consumers to make up for the B deficiency, and issued in a form which does not make its issue a further addition to the future price.

In short, when the "credit" idea requires a figure in accountancy, the social credit assumption is that there must be a fact corresponding to that figure, however physically impossible such a corresponding fact may be in the reality of things. Let me assure Mr. Douglas that the essential requirement in sound reckoning is the exact reverse—not that facts must be made to correspond with figures, but that figures must correspond with facts.

So far, therefore, as A payments made during the production of goods are concerned, nothing whatever remains of them, as actually surviving *consumer* power over any goods, by the time the final goods to which they are related as a price-component come into existence. They have been used up in *fact*, and their only survival is in the future price *figure*.

But although the future price thus stands for no *consumer* power over the goods when they come into final existence—although the consumer-power character of the A payments as effective power against *prices* has disappeared—a completely effective power over *the goods themselves* has entered into all this reckoning. For the goods, in actual fact, when they do make their appearance, do not come into being physically unappropriated. What has happened is that during the course of their production, all A power reckoned as being distributed against them has been transmuted into an exclusive property right of possession over them, *which is in fact the only power over them surviving in the final reckoning.*

All final products are delivered *in their entirety* into the property system. And since the A payments to consumers during their production is, in physical fact, a permit to consume already existing sustenance goods, what all this reckoning actually works out at in the reality of things is that the property system regularly obtains complete possession of the whole current flow of the world's output of new goods in return for releasing to the producers a sustenance supply of goods which have previously been appropriated into the property system in the same way.

Now, see how that is worked out in the reckoning. Since the "credit" idea is a complete reversal of the natural sequence of relationship in which production and consumption actually stand to one another—its reckoning of costs and prices always being an accountancy of the flow of consuming power as a flow in the direction of unconsumable, because non-existent, things—we may naturally expect to find the A+B theorem, based on such "credit" accountancy, completely reversed in relation to facts. Not reversed only in regard to the disappearance of its A payments, which in complete disregard of the facts it assumes to remain effective as consumer power against the A component in a future price; but also in regard to the B payments which it asserts to be non-effective as power over the goods unto whose prices they enter.

And so on scrutiny it proves to be. In actual fact, it is the B payments *only* which survive in active relation to the final products; for they are the payments by which the effective possession of all products is registered *as a property possession against any right of non-propertied consumers over them.*

The whole purpose of the reckoning is to prevent A payments from getting into the final price-reckoning as A payments. In the course of the accountancy by which costs are reckoned and prices created, *all A payments, in each stage of the producing process right away down from natural resources, are changed into B payments on their transmission into the next following stage; and it is only as B payments that they enter into the final reckoning*; the change in their character—from a consumer permit into a property claim—being completely effected in the cost-price accountancy by the time the final product stage is reached.

An illustrative case will make the essential facts as to this clearer than any amount of general description can do. Let us take Mr. Douglas's own case—the building of a factory which is later on to be used for making motor cars—and introduce into the process the B payments which Mr. Douglas left out.

A very great deal more has to be paid out than the £1,000 paid to the men. The association of owner and men constitutes an industrial organization for building, and it is only one small fragment in the producing process by which motor cars come into existence. Other industrial organizations, scattered by the thousand throughout the producing economy, have had to be at work before a brick can be laid or a window glazed or a water supply laid on. If you started out to catalogue all the requisite things that have to be assembled in the factory building from the preceding stages in this process of making motor cars, you would find that each one of them in its turn was produced by a similar assembly of components, and that things have had to come down to this synthesis in a factory from their origins in natural resources by thousands of contributory channels. And if to these actual components of the factory you add the services attached to them—the transport, the ramified activities for equipping each separate organization with the requisite machines and tools, and the basic power provision running through the whole process—you will begin to realize that Mr. Douglas was asking for a lot when he asked us to assume that materials were free; and possibly also to suspect that an attempt to reach an understanding about the relationship between purchasing power and final products which leaves all this out of account as something which would only introduce unnecessary complication may very easily fall short of any real understanding at all.

In fact there is no possible understanding, there are no data for real understanding, without considering the relationships of these separate organizations. For while each of them is only a fragment in a single producing economy, each of them is a separate self-contained property unit. Each of them, within its own organization, has to incur no cost and make no payment other than the A payment to its own servitors. But each of them has to make payments to the other organizations for its requisite materials and supplies. And when the requisite materials flow into the factory building organization, there flow in with them all the costs of all the other preceding organizations in respect of the materials and supplies; and the taking over of these costs at this stage in their flow into the ultimate prices of the motor cars is what constitutes the B payments which the owner of the factory building has to make to the other organizations.

Now what happens with regard to any one of these B payments made to other organizations is precisely what happens in all cases and at all stages; at every point at which the producing process is carried across from one stage to another on its way to final products. Let us, therefore, take a particular case, and see what happens when the owner in the factory building stage buys, say, the bricks required for his building.

He pays to the brick-making organization a lump sum—the price of the bricks—in which the whole of the costs incurred during the brick-making stage of the producing process are included, with the profit of the brick-making organization added; and that inclusive payment is a B payment.

But what are the costs incurred in the brick-making stage? None whatever, *within its own organization*, but the A payments made to its own servitors. For purposes of price-reckoning in regard to the final products, the ultimate motor cars, these A payments have therefore become B payments. The other costs which the brick-making organization had to incur and recover from the factory builder are simply transmitted costs, which the brick-making organization took over from other prior stages in the producing process; in which taking-over all previous A payments have in the same way already become a consolidated B payment and the sole component of the final price-reckoning. These transmitted "costs" cover everything up to that point; all materials, all profits, all rent and interest payments, and all the issue of sustenance goods assigned to the servitors in production, in all the organizations through which the materials have passed from natural resources down to the point at which they have been shaped into fitness for the brick-making stage of the producing process. Consolidated costs; in which no smallest fraction of an A payment remains in its character as a consumer claim against the prices of the forthcoming goods; all being merged into the single claim of ownership to appropriate the final product.

There is no need to pursue the thing into further detail. What happens in this instance of the transfer of materials from the brick-making to the factory-building organization is precisely what happens in every instance. Whenever any one of the thousands of separate organizations involved in any producing process passes its special contributory fragment of the general process on to the organizations that follow it in the producing sequence, this consolidation of all the preceding A payments into an inclusive B payment, as the only component of the price of the ultimate product, is effected.* The whole general flow of final products, over the entire range of industry, comes therefore into being, ready for market, with every claim against it eliminated—as extant purchasing power for equating the cost-

* As for the A payments made during the last stage of production, from which the ultimate product passes out of the producing system to the consumer, they also are used up by the time they are computed into the final price, being paid out to servitors for current sustenance. There may, however, be a fractional survival. But if the whole of the A payments made at this closing stage survived as purchasing power against the final price into which they are computed, they are in their entirety so fractional a part of the final price as to make very little difference. For example. There is a well-known woman's shoe which goes on to the market at 16s. 9d. the pair. One of the leading authorities in the national organization of the boot and shoe industry has been good enough to work out for me what proportion of that price is accounted for by the payments made for producing services in the factory. It amounts to 2s. 3d. the pair. Going to the other extreme, from a complex producing operation like shoe-making to a simple public service dealing directly with the consumer, the manager of one of our most important water-supply undertakings has given me corresponding figures for that industry. The total revenue received for supplies consumed works out at 14·40 pence per 1,000 gallons. The labour costs are 1·85 pence. From inquiries over a wide range of industries, it appears that over our general industrial activities, the costs incurred for producing services in the final product stage of the producing sequence average out at about three-ha'pence in the shilling of the price which the final product has to carry; and even that fractional price-component dwindles with every advance in the power-technique of manufacture.

price—other than the claim of which the B payment is the accountancy. And that claim is the claim of the property system to take the lot and hold it at the thus computed price against any consumer rights; the whole purpose of the accountancy being to ensure that no goods shall be permitted to escape from the property system to any consumer without thus rendering up in prices the property claim over them.

Throughout the whole reckoning, the accountancy registration of power over ultimate products is a registration of property rights and not of consumer rights at all; in strict conformity with the fact that each separate organization involved in the producing process is not primarily a producing unit but a property-ownership unit; a *business* unit, whose essential purpose is not to produce goods for use—it could attain that end much more effectively by *giving* the goods away into their appropriate use—but to obtain a price-payment for itself.

In other words, ownership secures, in return for releasing its special property-holding of fragments of a final product into their appropriate further use in the producing sequence, an equivalent property-holding in token form; and the "price" thus obtained represents current command for ownership over the current consumer goods it requires for its own use. Part of the price, of course, represents the similar property claims already made effective in the preceding organizations from which the materials came. But so far as the special utility values are concerned which each separate organization *adds* to the materials it thus took over, the upshot of the whole matter is that ownership, in each organization throughout the whole producing system, gets a complete use-and-consumption property claim upon any current consumer goods equivalent to that addition; at the sole cost of releasing the physically necessary sustenance allowance to the servitors of the organization.

The only real happening has been this current sustenance of the community by the passage of current goods into usage *in the class ratio denoted by the various payments entered as "costs"*; the entering of all such current consumption, whether by owners or by servitors, whether accounted as wages or profits or rents or what you will, into the aggregate of future prices being simply the accountancy by which rights to participate in the use and consumption of the forthcoming goods are allocated *in the same class ratio*—sustenance to such non-propertied people as the property system may find it necessary to employ in the yet further production which will then be going on, and the surplus to ownership. This class allocation is registered by the final consolidation of all costs, A and B alike, into a single B-payment component of the aggregate price of future goods; for while the B payments made by each separate property unit register the exchanges of goods with other property-ownership units, exchanges in which the money does not pass out of the property system at all, the consolidation of all costs into the B category registers the repayment to the property system of the money which had to be paid out momentarily to non-propertied servitors to enable them to take up their allotted sustenance. In the end, when any final product comes to market, the non-propertied class has neither the product nor the money with which to buy it; and can only obtain the money by again hiring itself out to render service to the property system in further production in return for a sustenance allowance of the final products of its previous service; and so on in a perpetual serial.

The situation, therefore, which A+B describes as arising when final products come to be marketed, is not the actual situation at all. It is a dream phantasy, in which the mere figures of a monetary accountancy are set up as the facts and realities of human living, and every actual movement of real goods, as that movement does in fact take place, is left out of account; a dream phantasy built up on the assumption that whatever movement of goods does take place must necessarily be only a mere shadow-accompaniment to the dance movement of the figures through the steps of the accountancy.

In the real movement of things, of course, actual

goods do not and cannot follow the movement of figures in any "credit" accountancy, which always assumes use and consumption to be related to goods which are not there for use or consumption; and the suggestion of any parallelism between the movement of goods into consumption and the movement of the figures of a credit accountancy into eventual prices brings you at once up against the absurd physical impossibilities which are fundamental in the "credit" conception of our economic life. What *is* related to the forthcoming goods in the price-computations of a credit accountancy is *the registering of a property title over them*; that and nothing whatever but that; as the accountancy itself testifies by its transformation of every price-component payment made during production into a B payment when the final cost-price is computed. The actual movement of consumer goods which does in fact take place is never for one moment governed by the money-accountancy; it is the money-accountancy which, in every movement of goods to which it is related, is governed by the property requirement as to what that movement shall be. The deliberate intention, *and the unvarying result*, of the whole procedure is to ensure that no consumer power over goods shall flow outside the property system beyond what is required to maintain the non-propertied class in working efficiency while the property system requires their services.

And that is the necessary relationship between money and the actual movement of goods *in a property economy*. If it works out, as in fact it invariably does, as an obstruction to the passage of goods to consumers, that is not in any way due to the money procedure, but to the essential property requirement that the passage of goods to the mass of non-propertied people shall be thus obstructed; a requirement which the money procedure merely registers and accounts. It is not by malevolence in monetary procedure, but in scrupulous fulfilment of the property requirements of which money is the accounting instrument, that it enters up the sustenance-consumption of the community as "costs," and prevents the issue of money to non-propertied consumers by any other channel than the disbursements made by the property system itself to its servitors in the course of further production; costs to be kept down with all possible rigour.

The "credit" accountancy on which A+B is based is wholly within this property framework; and cannot escape from the anti-consumer results which follow so long as production itself is carried on for the creation of property titles over goods. The new "social credit" money which it is proposed, on the basis of the A+B reasoning, to issue direct to consumers remains—and within a property economy must remain—related to *price* claims. It is to be issued as *purchasing power*. Its operative function is to be the satisfaction of the price claims; i.e. to enable the property system to make its claim over products effective through prices. It is to operate in that respect precisely as ordinary property-token money operates; as power *for the receiver of the price* over a general goods equivalent of the special property he gives up for it. And with that creation of a duplicated claim over all issued products against the consumer claim which the issue of the new money was intended to establish, it becomes a mere inflation of the ordinary property-token money issue, and as useless to consumers as all inflation is. No money issued within a property economy for the purpose of meeting price claims over goods can escape from that dilemma: the moment the price is paid the money becomes a duplicated purchasing power against the same output of goods, and reverts to the ordinary property-token money type in inflation.

It could only escape from this dilemma and become operative as a real consumer claim on goods by immediate cancellation; by making it a simple ticket for goods with no further money-validity attached to it after the consumer has presented it and received the goods for it. And since that would obviously be a process of smashing the property system by handing its property out to consumers for nothing, the idea of putting it into operation within a property-producing economy is inherently absurd.

The "credit" accountancy of costs and prices cannot be made to function as a consumer accountancy; for the simple and sufficient reason that it is only within a property economy, and as an assertion of power over goods against the consumer, that any price claim gets into the reckoning at all, or that an accountancy of the current sustenance of human life as a cost of producing goods has any meaning whatever.

For Product Safety Concerns and Information please contact our EU representative GPSR@taylorandfrancis.com
Taylor & Francis Verlag GmbH, Kaufingerstraße 24, 80331 München, Germany

www.ingramcontent.com/pod-product-compliance
Ingram Content Group UK Ltd.
Pitfield, Milton Keynes, MK11 3LW, UK
UKHW022157190926
475702UK00003B/66

* 9 7 8 1 1 3 8 8 3 2 7 5 6 *